Led by a Thread

Following God's Call to Priesthood

DAVID FORRESTER

A Redemptorist Publication

Published by **Redemptorist Publications**
A Registered Charity limited by guarantee. Registered in England 3261721.

Copyright © David Forrester, 2009

First published September 2009

Layout by Peena Lad
Cover design by Rosemarie Pink

ISBN 978-0-85231-367-1

A CIP catalogue record for this book is available from the British Library

Printed by Bishops Printers Limited, Portsmouth PO6 1RU

Redemptorist
P U B L I C A T I O N S
Alphonsus House Chawton Hampshire GU34 3HQ
Telephone 01420 88222 Fax 01420 88805
rp@rpbooks.co.uk   www.rpbooks.co.uk

In memory of Tony Battle
1942–2005

Something is very gently,
invisibly, silently,
pulling at me – a thread
or net of threads
finer than cobweb and as
elastic... Not fear
but a stirring
of wonder makes me
catch my breath when I feel
the tug of it when I thought
it had loosened itself and gone.

Denise Levertov, "The Thread", in *Denise Levertov Poems 1960 – 1967*
(New York: New Directions Publishing Corp, 1984).
Reproduced by permission of Pollinger Limited.

Introduction

It is almost a cliché to describe life in present-day Britain as post-Christian. It certainly would seem to be becoming increasingly secular, materialistic and hedonistic, with huge gaps between the lives of the rich and the poor. All these things leave little room for the life of the Spirit.

The massive decline in numbers attending Mass, leading to either the closure or amalgamation of parishes, only adds to the gloom. Under the circumstances, some people ask, is it any wonder that fewer men and women are offering themselves for the religious life, or young men for the diocesan priesthood?

To be a Roman Catholic priest in England in the twenty-first century is no joke. Obviously in England today priests no longer face persecution of the kind experienced by priests in the reign of Elizabeth I, when one could be arrested, hanged, drawn and quartered simply for being a priest. Today a priest faces a quite different set of difficulties, namely indifference and being regarded and treated as irrelevant, a relic of the past.

As though this were not enough, a priest of today has to contend with problems within the Church, such as the constant questioning of such things as the use of contraception, issues of life and death such as abortion and euthanasia, clerical celibacy and the place of women in the Church. And this is not to mention how priesthood has become tainted and associated in the minds of many with the scandal of child abuse.

So why should any man offer himself these days for the Catholic priesthood?

This small book has been written with the purpose of illustrating that the life of a Catholic priest today is not all gloom and doom. Challenging, sometimes frustrating – yes, but ultimately utterly fulfilling.

It has also been written in a spirit of optimism and without any regrets whatsoever, despite any difficulties experienced along the way. I have endeavoured to show that the vocation to priesthood is one that young men of today can embrace with the certainty that they are not only needed but called and deeply loved by God and those he entrusts to their care.

I would like to express my appreciation of the following people at Redemptorist Publications: Andrew Lyon, Caroline Dickerson and Peter Edwards, who so professionally edited my manuscript, and Fr Denis McBride C.Ss.R., who kick-started the process of publication in the very beginning.

Contents

1. Early days   9

2. Conversion   24

3. Spiritual direction   35

4. The English College, Rome   42

5. Parish life   57

6. Oxford chaplain   79

7. Eton   89

8. A priest in residence   108

Epilogue   118

1

Early days

At first I was not aware of my good fortune at being born into this particular family, consisting of a mother and father and a brother twelve years older than me. My mother was forty-three when I was born and my father forty-four. In other words, throughout my childhood my parents seemed rather old compared to those of my friends and I might as well have been an only child, my brother being that much older than myself, away at boarding school and at home only during the school holidays. It was years before I learnt that my mother had run away from home during the First World War in order to become a nurse, her parents not approving of young women going out to work. Then, as a Sister in charge of a ward at a large city hospital, given over at that time to tending to the needs of wounded soldiers, she first met my father and fell in love. The story handed down in the family is that my father, on first setting eyes on my mother, declared to the soldier in the next bed that that was the woman he intended to marry. And he did.

My mother was small, intuitive and dynamic; my father tall, highly intelligent and lazy. He would do anything to avoid responsibilities and so my mother was forced to shoulder them and to take all decisions. He also had a roving eye and my childhood was often punctured by rows between my parents, with my mother being left in tears by my father's infidelities. When I was born it was the mid 1930s and a time in England when most people, with memories of the First World War, refused to imagine that a catastrophe in the form of Nazism would soon change the world for ever.

For a child growing up in such a world, however, life seemed like one long summer. Born in a small red-brick town, called Rushden in Northamptonshire, a place with no pretensions to beauty and whose chief claim to fame lay in its boot and shoe factories and the fact that the novelist H.E. Bates had once lived there, I revelled in the freedom afforded me by the fact that both my parents went out to work. My mother became a district nurse and midwife and my father was employed in John White's, a well-known shoemaking factory.

During those hours when neither of my parents was at home, I was left in the care of a woman known to everyone as Auntie Hilda, a woman who had a huge and natural understanding of children. To my child's eye Auntie Hilda looked like a large Gypsy woman. I couldn't understand how someone could have such jet-black hair and dark skin. To me she was both mysterious and utterly understanding of a child's thoughts and needs. It was to Auntie Hilda that I immediately turned for help whenever I was in trouble or when I felt sick. She ran what today would be regarded as an unofficial playschool, but she ran it on lines that today would be thought of as highly unorthodox and a nightmare to health and safety officials. Hilda's teenage daughter, for example, was a member of a tap-dancing troupe for which Hilda made all the costumes. Not only did Hilda take all the children in her care, including me, to the troupe's rehearsals, but she encouraged us to dress up in the costumes she was making and learn the troupe's dance steps and moves. Another of her activities was the making of highly decorated wedding cakes, for which she sought our opinions as to their design and taste. Later her house became a haven for children evacuated from London.

Being left at Auntie Hilda's by my parents was always exciting and a learning activity for a child. During the festive season of Christmas she taught us all how to make Christmas decorations and cards and helped us to choose presents for our friends. Her house was a refuge for everyone I knew. Her husband, Albert, said very little but was invariably there in the background. Uncle Albert, as we called him, was a mystery figure for a child. He sat in his armchair with his hair glistening with Brylcreem and carefully parted in the middle, a tear permanently in his left eye and an enigmatic smile on his face. We all knew him as the man who had lost a leg in the First World War.

On Sunday mornings, although a baptised member of the Church of England, I was taken to the Salvation Army for Sunday school by three serious-minded middle-aged spinsters. Faith is a gift from God and looking back I now trace the first beginnings of my growth in the faith to this time. It was at the Salvation Army that I was to learn all about the Old Testament patriarchs and New Testament parables during lessons from teachers using, to my eyes, wonderful visual aids. I particularly enjoyed their account of Jonah and the whale, which they illustrated by the use of a tank full of water with toy ships, fish and other sea creatures floating in the water, and at other times their use of a large sand tray, with rocks, toy animals and figures to explain, for instance, the parable of the Good Samaritan. It was at the Salvation Army too that it was discovered that I apparently had a remarkable boy-soprano singing voice, something that I simply accepted as part of myself and wondered what all the fuss was about, except that it set me apart from other boys of my age. It was, however, something I valued, and I became extremely distressed when it later naturally broke as I grew older.

At that time I was too young to appreciate that already our family lifestyle at home was somewhat different from that of the majority of the children in my primary school a few streets away – different in the sense of not fitting into any usual category. Firstly my parents, or rather my mother, had commissioned the design and building of our home and had employed a nanny to look after me up to the age of five. How she could afford to do such things never crossed my mind. Secondly my parents were among the few people I knew to own a car, and thirdly I knew no one who had a brother or sister at boarding school.

I did realise, however, that my aunts and uncles on both sides were wonderfully different from the relatives of my friends. I first began to appreciate how unusual my family was when, after World War II, when I was thirteen, my parents sent me alone to New York to stay with friends of theirs for a holiday. It was before the age of jet planes and the flight in an aeroplane with propellers took eighteen hours, landing first at

Shannon in Ireland and then at Gander in Newfoundland. My holiday featured in all the local newspapers as something highly unusual, and so it was at that time.

On my father's side I had nine uncles and aunts, all of whom were either publicans or somehow connected with the brewing industry, my father being the exception. Too young to be allowed in, I spent a great deal of my early childhood sitting on the doorsteps of public houses run by relatives. On my mother's side I had one uncle who as a barrister had gone to India to practise the law and had married a beautiful Indian Jewish woman named Sally Gubbay; another uncle who had moved to South Africa to become the manager of a bank; and an aunt who owned and ran her own drapery shop in Derby. The only cousin I ever came to know was the only child of my Indian aunt, and approximately my own age. During his teenage years he trained as a ballet dancer and later became a well-known stage and costume designer. His name was David Walker.

In those days to have an Indian aunt seemed highly exotic. Whenever we visited my aunt I recall the house being full of smells that were unfamiliar to me at the time, which I now identify as the aroma of either curry or fried rice; and I remember my aunt chatting noisily to her friends in a language unknown to me, which I now realise must have been either Hindi or Urdu.

My other aunt, my mother's younger sister, Ethel, the one who owned a draper's shop in Derby, was in the eyes of a child also extraordinary, but married to a man who was so ordinary and self-effacing that his regular bowler hat and pipe seemed more real than his personality. All he lived for was my aunt. His name was Basil. Every evening after the shop was closed, my aunt and uncle went to a fashionable bar in the centre of Derby called The Saint James, or Jimmy's for short. There they socialised, told stories, laughed and joked with their friends; when I was visiting them, I sat outside in the car.

Early on in their marriage they decided never to have children. In later life they went on cruises together to foreign parts, which in those days seemed highly glamorous, and, instead of children, they kept a massive dog. My cousin David and I loved staying with our Aunt Ethel. To us she was the epitome of fashion, fun and high living; we easily joined in the adoration given her by our Uncle Basil. Sadly, years later, in old age and widowhood, she put a plastic bag over her head and killed herself.

This blissful childhood world, of seaside holidays at Bournemouth, or Brancaster on the Norfolk coast, of car trips in our small Austin Seven (with me in the back seat on our way to visit either my brother at boarding school at Dover or my aunt in Derby) and long hours on summer evenings spent accompanying my father as he played bowls with his friends from work, suddenly came to an end with the outbreak of war with Germany and, in particular, on the day a German bomb landed on my primary school.

Up to that point I had sometimes wondered whether my father actually loved me. One of my earliest memories is of my mother frequently informing me that, when she was found to be pregnant with me at forty-three, my father had urged her to have an abortion, but she had refused, repeating like a mantra that she "might be turning the greatest blessing into the greatest curse". At the time it did not seem strange that she should tell me this, but it certainly made me wonder whether my father loved me. And then the bomb fell.

I was five when the war began and it appeared not to impinge much on my life except for sweet rationing and the increasingly frequent routine at home of sleeping in a shelter under the stairs whenever the sirens went off. Actually I found this exciting, with my parents and neighbours crowded round, all drinking tea and exchanging stories, while I lay on a mattress pretending to be asleep. Meanwhile at school we practised hiding under our desks whenever an air raid seemed imminent. Then one day it was the real thing.

An enemy bomber being chased by several British planes needed to get up speed, so its pilot decided to drop its load as quickly as possible. At least one bomb landed on my primary school, in the classroom next to mine. I recall a huge bang and then looking up and thinking that it was taking a long time for the ceiling to fall down; and then, later, squatting under my desk amidst all the dust and debris. I found the whole experience somehow surreal and even exciting. That was until I realised that probably some of my friends in the next room must have been killed. Indeed my closest friend at the time was one of them.

Very shortly after this there was a loud knocking at the classroom door and the sound of parents arriving at the school in search of their children. Among them and clearly the loudest was my father, a fact that made me leap up and run towards the door. As my father entered the damaged room he saw me immediately, hoisted me on his shoulders and carried me home through the streets crowded with people converging on the school. As I sat up high, with blackened face from the dust of the debris, and looked down smiling at everyone as they passed, I realised that my father must love me to have been the first to reach the school and to look for me.

Soon afterwards we moved to the comparative safety of a village in the country where, with both my parents going out to work, the freedom afforded me allowed me to spend long hours roaming the fields, climbing trees and playing in hayricks with my friends. On Sundays I was taken by my mother to worship in the local Anglican church and my ties with the Salvation Army came to an end. Three years later, when I was nine, I was sent to a boarding school, which had been evacuated because of the war to a former hotel, standing on the cliffs at Saunton Sands, looking out to the Atlantic Ocean in north Devon.

Initially boarding school was both a revelation and a nightmare. Hitherto I had heard only vaguely of such places. The shock of being sent away from home was made worse by the fact that I was sent to a military boarding school, the only one in England, called the Duke of York's Royal Military School, founded in 1803 by the so-called grand old Duke of York, the one who was scorned – as the old song says – for having marched his men to the top of the hill and down again.

All the staff at the school either had been or were still officers or non-commissioned officers in the army. Our school uniform consisted of khaki jackets with many brass buttons, which had to be kept shining brightly, short trousers, and boots which also needed to be kept constantly polished. We were addressed by our surnames and each given a number, which was stamped on all our clothing. We rose at 6.45 every morning to the sound of a bugle playing reveille, after which we washed, rolled up our bedclothes, swept the dormitory and were then marched off to breakfast. After that we attended lessons in army huts hastily erected along the cliffs beside the former hotel.

On Saturdays there was the regimental sergeant major's parade, during which we were inspected from top to bottom, spent at least an hour drilling up and down and listened to endless tirades from him about how horribly slack we were. On wet days when we could not parade we sat learning the history and traditions of all the major regiments in the British army. On Sundays we had church parade before attending compulsory services in the morning and evening conducted by an army chaplain. It was the evening service that I recall most, for it was then that the chaplain read to us from John Bunyan's *Pilgrim's Progress*. I have never forgotten the book's chief character, Christian, with whom I was able to identify and find consolation.

All this took place against the backcloth of the unending sound of the sea and overlooking a beach five miles long, bordering the Atlantic Ocean on the north Devon coast. It was on this same beach and during my time there that Michael Powell and Emeric Pressburger directed scenes for their noteworthy film *A Matter of Life and Death*, which more than alluded to the relation between heaven and earth.

The only reason I was sent by my parents to such a school was because my brother had been there before me, though I doubt whether this would have been a sufficient reason if it had been known how much bullying and abuse of the younger boys by the older ones took place.

Just as the advent of war had meant for me the end of childhood happiness, so boarding school meant the end of innocence. In a relatively short time, however, I adapted to this new way of life and indeed eventually grew to enjoy it. Most of all it alleviated my frequent loneliness at being virtually an only child, with my brother now overseas fighting the Germans in Italy. He was to be killed in action in the last year of the war, a tragedy from which neither of my parents ever fully recovered.

Perhaps the most significant event that occurred to me during my years at boarding school was a spiritual experience I had at the age of nine. Hitherto I had simply taken the existence of God for granted, having as one of my earliest memories that of watching my mother kneeling every night by her bed to say her prayers, a practice she maintained to the last years of her life. At other times, from attending Sunday school at the local Salvation Army in my home town, I had become familiar, as I said earlier, with the stories of the patriarchs in the Old Testament and the parables in the New Testament.

On this occasion, however, as I was walking all alone along the sandy beach in front of the school at the edge of the sea, and wondering why my parents had sent me away to boarding school, I suddenly became aware of the fact I was not alone, but in the actual presence of God. I have no idea how I knew this nor did I think of the experience as strange, but I suddenly seemed to be bathed in intense light and deeply comforted by the knowledge that God was addressing me. I gathered that he would always be at my side watching over me, including those occasions when I might behave as though he did not exist.

One of the most immediate effects of this encounter was to make me appreciate that listening in prayer, as distinct from uttering words (usually at this stage in the form of petitionary prayers), was an important part of praying. Thereafter whenever I prayed, I would often deliberately pause in order to try to discern whatever God had to say. This was especially true of times of crisis. It was done quite naturally and in a matter-of-fact way, without show or fuss and certainly without informing other people. Gradually as I grew up, and through trial and error, I also learnt how to differentiate between when God was speaking and when I was merely talking interiorly to myself. Years later when I had occasion either to write or speak about prayer, I would emphasise the crucial difference between listening, in other words giving God one's complete attention, and merely hearing.

Looking back to the time when I was nine and knowing now how other young children often behave, I am amazed how straightforwardly they often behave in the face of spiritual experiences, including

16

encounters with God. It is sad that later in life such acceptance is frequently replaced by scepticism and even doubt.

Since that encounter on the beach at Saunton Sands, I have never once doubted God's existence, even on those occasions when my conduct has been selfish and clearly opposed to his will; and indeed my greatest fear ever since that day has been that this awareness of God would one day disappear. The experience changed my life in ways that initially I didn't realise. My everyday behaviour did not radically alter, but thereafter both boys and staff at the school quietly seemed to take it for granted that I would one day be a priest. I kept this experience on the beach a complete secret until I reached my thirties.

It was only later in the seminary, and even later after writing of this experience in the Jesuit magazine *The Way*, that I learned that such experiences are not unusual, and that those who have them tend not to broadcast the fact, either because they consider them extremely precious or so as not to be thought odd. Bishop Anthony Emery, the Bishop of Portsmouth at one time, for example, once gently informed me that he had had a similar experience as a child to that which I had on that north Devon beach.

This spiritual awareness in my early years was soon after accompanied in my adolescence by a massive need for affection and friendship. Indeed from then until I reached maturity my life seemed to be one continual search for outlets for my often-conflicting emotions. Many people who lived through the war years speak of that time not only as one of constant danger but as a time when they allowed their feelings full play. It was as though they felt that, because they might die at any moment either in warfare or from air raids, they should live life to the full while they had the opportunity. Life at boarding school mirrored this unspoken tendency among the adults.

As a small boy, one moment I might be praying in earnest for my brother and the men under his command fighting in Italy, the next I would be daydreaming about a Jewish girl – one of the many evacuees in the care of Auntie Hilda back home. As the school was an all-male establishment miles from the nearest town, girls were only ever encountered in the holidays or watched from afar on the silver screen, when we were watching films on a Saturday evening in the school gymnasium. The absence of my parents and of girls was among the chief privations of boarding-school life in wartime, not to mention food rationing and other shortages. With the ending of hostilities, however, my school returned to its pre-war premises on the so-called white cliffs of Dover, made famous in the war in the well-known song sung by Vera Lynn.

It was when I turned seventeen and was in the Lower Sixth that I discovered the existence of the Catholic Church. Although there were Catholics at the school and they had their own small chapel where they went on Sundays, they always struck me as odd and their activities and practices never merited attention, until that day, that is, when a woman member of staff surreptitiously handed me a book as she was passing and told me to read it. I never found out why she did this.

Initially I thought it was because someone had told her I was considering becoming a Church of England priest and then I imagined it may have been because I was gradually becoming known as someone who was making his mark by winning school prizes in history. Whatever the reason for the teacher handing me that book, whose title now escapes me, it marked another milestone in my religious development. As I read it, the effect was of scales falling from before my eyes.

This awareness of the existence of the Catholic Church coincided with summer visits, arranged by the school authorities, to a family in Belgium in order to learn French. There I first began visiting Catholic churches, feeling drawn to a liturgy which in those days was in Latin, and devotion to such saints in particular as Thérèse of Lisieux. Unconsciously I was becoming increasingly aware of the value of the numinous in worship. These were new and exciting discoveries for an adolescent such as myself, hitherto acquainted only with either low Church of England or Salvation Army worship.

Up to this point my prayer life had centred solely on the person of Jesus Christ, with an almost evangelical emphasis being placed on the salvation he had won for us by his death on the cross and subsequent resurrection. Clearly this was a result of my early days in the Salvation Army. Now, however, my growing awareness of the richness of Catholic worship, resulting from my visits to Belgium and my reading of the book on Catholicism handed me by the teacher, was having the effect of leaving me dissatisfied with the way I was praying. In my worship too I wanted more than stress being placed solely on Christ's redemptive work as depicted in the scriptures, hugely important though this was. I felt instinctively that both my worship and my prayer life were vital but grounded on too narrow a basis.

As a practising Christian and a budding historian, one of my major preoccupations also became that of ensuring that I belonged to the Church originally founded by Christ. After reading the book handed me by the teacher I began to have serious doubts as to whether the Church of England fell into this category. I began questioning whether it truly could trace its roots back to apostolic times and whether its bishops could actually trace their succession back in time to the twelve apostles. Above all, I was plagued with doubts as to whether one could be a true member of the Church founded by Christ unless one was in communion with the Pope, the successor of Peter, the apostle specifically installed by Christ as leader of the twelve.

Much as I appreciated the holy lives of many Anglicans, adored the prayers and language of the Book of Common Prayer, rejoiced in a liturgy so beautifully celebrated, especially when found in cathedrals throughout the land, my personal feeling was that I could find no real evidence for believing that it was not simply a nationally established church, divorced from Rome and constructed by Cranmer on the orders of Henry VIII in the sixteenth century. In view of this, and despite the Catholic Church's man-made failings and blemishes recorded in history, I felt cut off from the still living, vibrant organism founded by Christ and kept alive by the Holy Spirit in the Catholic Church.

Soon after coming to this conclusion, I was reading John Henry Newman's *Apologia Pro Vita Sua*, his defence and explanation of his conversion to Catholicism. Shortly after that I came across Thomas Merton's autobiography, *The Seven Storey Mountain*. This book, which created a publishing stir when it first appeared in 1948, was the account of a talented young man's journey from non-belief and a promiscuous way of life to conversion to Catholicism and entry into an enclosed Trappist monastery. It certainly had me hooked. I knew then that I had no choice but to become a Catholic. This realisation, however, was merely the beginning of a decade of struggle within my family.

It is difficult to describe the extent of my parents' hostility when I informed them that I wished to become a Catholic. Both of them had been born and brought up as God-fearing practising Protestants in the 1890s, the last years of Queen Victoria's reign. One of my earliest memories was of staying with one of my father's sisters and, while lying in bed, reading framed biblical texts hanging on the walls of the bedroom. Both my parents came from totally anti-Catholic backgrounds, not unusual for their generation, complete with horror stories about Bloody Mary, the Spanish Armada and the Gunpowder Plot. They could think of nothing worse than becoming a Catholic. I argued that it was not as if I wanted to become a communist but simply a better Christian, but they would not listen. My father's hostility took the form of silent consternation and my mother's that of endless, sometimes hysterical, tears and unreason. The school holidays were full of arguments, rows, recriminations, and a breakdown in real communication between them and me.

Then, when I resigned from the school chapel choir on the grounds that I no longer believed the Church of England to be part of the Catholic Church, the controversy became a matter for the school authorities. I was ordered to report to the school commandant and account for my behaviour. When I stood to attention before this full colonel, having been marched into his office by the regimental sergeant major, he demanded an explanation. To this day I can still recall his reaction when I informed him that I wished to become a Catholic.

"You have caught Roman fever," he said. "You will get over it, now get back in the choir!"

Obviously I did not get over it and instead began cycling to Catholic churches in the holidays and spending an increasing amount of time praying before the Blessed Sacrament.

It was about this time that I also set my heart on going to Oxford to study history. This was a subject that a taskmaster of a teacher at the school had encouraged me to become passionately interested in. Still today I can recall his reasons for driving me to study history as he did. Firstly, he would tell me that a study of history enables a person to discover how human beings over the centuries have organised their lives, both individually and collectively, and, if such a study also incorporates research into the beliefs, traditions and value systems of peoples in different historical periods and civilisations, it enhances a student's perceptive and judgemental abilities. Secondly, he would insist that history, of necessity, promotes a student's analytical and critical skills, requiring him or her to assess the value of evidence and ultimately come to conclusions, whatever period of history and whatever type of society is being investigated. He was convinced that history was for a nation what memory was to an individual, and he would demand to know how a person could effectively function without a memory.

Unfortunately this decision of mine to go to university did not meet with the approval of the school commandant. It had always been the tradition until then that once a boy was in the sixth form, he would make the regular army his career by first seeking entry to Sandhurst, the military college for the training of young officers. To the amazement of the commandant, however, four of us decided otherwise, so once again I found myself with the others standing before the colonel.

"What is this I hear about you all wishing to go to university? Is it true?" he demanded.

To this, while standing to attention and looking straight ahead, we all replied together, "Yes, Sir."

"And which university do you wish to attend?" he then asked each of us in turn, beginning with the head boy.

"Oxford, Sir," he replied, as did I. The second said "Cambridge" and the third "Birmingham". (This last choice snobbishly appalled the rest of us and seemed to dismay the colonel even further.)

By now the colonel was furiously red in the face. He managed to tell us that there was nothing he could do to prevent us applying, but that the school would give us no help whatsoever with our applications. We had to do all the running ourselves. To everyone's surprise, in the event we all got into the university of our choice, but first we all had to complete our two years of compulsory national service in the army.

It was also when I was seventeen that I fell in love for the first time. It was with the Jewish girl I had first met at Auntie Hilda's, had known for several years by then, and frequently daydreamed about. We even became engaged to marry a year later, but both her parents and mine disapproved of the relationship, applied pressure on us to break it up and forbade us to write to or see each other ever again. Obviously we took no notice and indeed continued to meet secretly and correspond with each other by sending letters via Auntie Hilda the whole time I was in the army undergoing my two years' military service.

In my second term at university, after completing my military service, however, and without warning, suddenly I received no more letters. I visited Auntie Hilda to find out why and, instead of giving me an explanation, she produced a photograph which showed the girl I loved coming down the steps of a synagogue in a wedding dress and on the arm of a young man I did not know. The girl and I never met or spoke to each other ever again.

After nine years of military boarding school, the regular army by comparison seemed almost slack and the two years of compulsory national service that I spent in it would today be termed a doddle. After ten weeks of basic training with the Royal Artillery at Oswestry in Shropshire, I was selected and sent to Eaton Hall Officer Cadet School at Chester and, from there, was posted as a second lieutenant to Feltham in Middlesex for the remainder of my military service.

On the whole I considered national service a useful experience, though much of it seemed a waste of time. Whenever I was bored I would search out the nearest Catholic church and go there to pray. I even began to take instructions in the Catholic faith from a priest, but after a few weeks I told him that if he had been giving me lessons in communism I would by then have become an ardent communist. I felt that he was indoctrinating me. Even so I continued to haunt Catholic churches wherever I found myself, drawn by their atmosphere, which seemed to encourage one to pray.

The event that I most often recall of those two years in the army was participating in what was known as Battle Camp on Dartmoor in winter. There we performed manoeuvres using live ammunition and sleeping outdoors in trenches in the freezing cold. For me the experience was rendered more memorable by the fact that the previous week I had fallen seriously ill with influenza. When granted a week's leave before leaving for Dartmoor, I had hastened to my Aunt Ethel in Derby. I had every confidence that she would know how to cure me, otherwise my passing out as an officer would be delayed.

On my arrival my aunt took my temperature, immediately ordered me to bed and piled it high with several blankets. She handed me a full bottle of rum and told me to drink it. The following few days were simply a blur, but I'm told they consisted of me sweating considerably and expelling the flu with this mixture of alcohol and heat. I returned to Chester extremely weak and as white as a sheet, but cured of flu. I have hated rum and the smell of it ever since.

Towards the end of my national service my father died of cancer. When I went to identify his body in the hospital it was the first time I had ever seen a dead body. What struck me most was how much it resembled an empty shell. My father was clearly no longer there. The experience confirmed my belief in the existence of the soul.

When I was demobilised in 1954 and before going to Oxford University, I decided to go to Paris. After nine years of military boarding school and two years in the army, I felt I needed somehow to start completely afresh and get everything military out of my system.

2

Conversion

In many ways Paris was exactly what I was looking for. I was twenty years old and desperate to broaden my horizons after the constrictions of boarding school and army life. I told myself that I needed something completely different. Paris for me stood for the world of art and culture and was the home of such post-war intellectuals as Jean-Paul Sartre and Simone de Beauvoir, whose novel *Les Mandarins*, with its mixture of existentialist philosophy, politics and human relationships, had become my Bible. Paris also represented for me the period of history I had studied so intensely – the French Revolution and the Napoleonic era. But where was I to start?

After checking into a modest hotel overlooking the Seine and arming myself with a serious guidebook, I began visiting all the major places recommended, such as Notre Dame, the Tuileries garden, Montmartre and so on. I walked everywhere and devoured all the sights like a person who had not eaten for months, but after three or four days not only were my feet beginning to blister and my head to ache in the summer heat, but I began to feel lonely. Paris might be everything one reads about it, but I needed someone to share its beauty with. So far I had spoken to no one except the concierge at the hotel.

It was this lack of a companion that prompted me to purchase some French clothes and to have my hair cut in a crew cut. Perhaps then, I thought, I shall look less like a foreigner. Even so it made little difference. After I changed my appearance the only person who came up and spoke to me was an Englishman seeking directions to the Arc de Triomphe in execrable French. I told him that if he spoke in English I would understand him better, at which he stormed off in a temper. Finally, feeling very low and wondering if I should return to England, I decided to improve my knowledge of art at least by first visiting the Louvre before leaving for home.

The Louvre that morning was not exactly empty but neither was it full. I decided to do things methodically and begin by examining the pictures in the Byzantine gallery and then steadily work my way through the rooms devoted to the paintings of subsequent centuries to the present day. Within minutes of starting this, however, I wondered whether it might have been better if I had begun my study the other way round. I thought this as I stood before a huge golden icon painted in a way that hitherto I had not encountered. The saints it showed seemed misshapen and out of proportion and perspective. I had no idea how to view the icon in order to obtain the effect the artist intended.

It was while I was trying to puzzle this out that a cultured masculine voice to my left asked in impeccable French if I had a problem with the picture before me. Without turning to see whose voice it was, I replied, also in French, that I hadn't a clue what the artist was trying to convey. Only after the person told me to look at this part of the painting and then that, and advised me of the meaning and purpose of icons in general, did I begin gradually to understand. It was also then that I turned to thank whoever it was that had become my first teacher in art history and appreciation.

To my left stood a tall young man who must have been only three or four years older than myself, but from the worldly point of view seemed much older. He was dark, good looking, immaculately dressed and, from all that he obviously knew about art, clearly highly educated. He introduced himself as being not French but an Italian named Piero Bozzetti.

From the Byzantine gallery he took me to the galleries devoted to the Renaissance and such artists as Giovanni Bellini and Titian, and after that to those of the eighteenth century and the paintings of Canaletto. Finally by lunchtime we reached the pictures of the twentieth century.

By then I had learnt so much that I was truly amazed. I had also learnt that my guide was a schoolmaster. Later he was to become first an art critic and then the cultural attaché in one of his country's most important embassies abroad.

It was at this point that he said that he had to leave to have lunch at the house of the friends with whom he was staying. He informed me, however, that in the afternoon he intended to see an exhibition of Cézanne's paintings at the Musée de l'Orangerie and asked if I would like to accompany him and learn about Impressionist paintings. In my eagerness to deepen my knowledge of art even more and from such a skilled teacher, I obviously said that I would and we agreed to meet at the gallery a couple of hours later.

That afternoon, as I imbibed all that the Italian taught me about Impressionism, I reflected that that day had been all that I had sought and hoped for by visiting Paris. It allowed me to put memories of boarding school and the army behind me. It seemingly opened up avenues I knew to exist but had not known how to explore and I felt ready to return home.

At the end of that day of learning all about art, however, my Italian friend informed me that the following afternoon he intended to visit the zoo and asked if I would like to accompany him. This made me curious. Would he teach me as much about the animal world as he had of art?

The next afternoon he gave me the equivalent of a masterclass on every animal in the zoo. He backed up all this information with evident knowledge of birds, trees and plants. In other words he opened my eyes yet again, only this time to the world of nature in all its forms. I had never previously met anyone so knowledgeable. My time in Paris was an excellent preparation for Oxford.

A day or so later I caught the train and ferry to England. During subsequent years Piero Bozzetti and I kept in touch by letter and observed each other's progress, little realising that from time to time in the future our paths would cross again at significant moments in the lives of both of us. Today, after ending his career as his country's cultural attaché to the United States, he is the friend I have known the longest and to this day, now in old age, he remains passionately interested in the world and people around him.

Oxford in the 1950s still retained more than a few of the aspects of university life that featured so much in Evelyn Waugh's novel *Brideshead Revisited.* Colleges were still single-sex, all undergraduates still had their own college servant, a degree of formal attire was still required at dinner in the evenings and all students had to be in their college by midnight each night. Patrolling the streets of Oxford after midnight were the equivalent of university police known as the proctors, dressed in formal gowns and hoods, followed by two men in bowler hats known as bulldogs. It was the latter's job to chase and apprehend any undergraduates found outside their college after midnight and demand to know their business. The lucky ones, including me, were those who knew how to scale the walls of their college, which in my case was Keble, and so elude being arrested.

The majority of male undergraduates at that time had all done their two years of national service before coming up and were simply eager now to enjoy life as much as possible. As a consequence – after we had devoted a certain amount of time each day to study in preparation for the weekly tutorial – parties, balls, trips to the cinema or theatre and serious drinking were usually the order of the day. In the case of those who had risked their lives in the Korean War during their national service, this seemed entirely excusable. Afternoons in Trinity, or summer, term were frequently spent punting with friends on the River Cherwell, drinking wine and playing gramophone records as we flowed along. During the vacations many of us secretly took holiday jobs (something forbidden by the university authorities) in order to gain money for travel on the continent afterwards. It was for this reason that I and a friend from my college obtained employment each July in a pea-canning factory in Lowestoft. There my eyes were first opened to the lives of working-class women factory workers, an experience that helped turn my political inclinations in a left-wing direction.

In my second year at Oxford I once again, only more seriously this time, began to receive instruction in Catholicism from a Dominican at Blackfriars close to my college. Until then I had been attending daily Anglican services in the college chapel, but they left me strangely unfulfilled and now I stopped. This was noticed by the head of my college, Dr Harry Carpenter, a scholarly and ascetic high Church of England clergyman, who subsequently became the Bishop of Oxford. He sent for me and, when I told him that I intended to become a Catholic, sat me down and proceeded to give me the equivalent of a tutorial lasting two and a half hours on the evils of Rome.

What Warden Carpenter failed to take into account was that what had drawn me to the Catholic faith and accounted for my frequent visiting of Catholic churches from my teenage years onwards was more than just a knowledge of history and theological debate. What kept drawing me to Catholicism was its belief in the Real Presence of Christ in the sacrament of the Eucharist. What is more, although as yet I could not receive this sacrament, I could at least spend time praying before the tabernacle to be found in every Catholic church, in which consecrated hosts, left over from the Eucharist, were retained, both to be taken to those who were sick and to encourage devotion to Christ. The red light indicating the Real Presence constantly drew me, in much the manner indicated by Evelyn Waugh in his novel *Brideshead Revisited*, which I was assiduously reading during my undergraduate days.

Despite Warden Carpenter's warnings, I persisted in my intentions, an action that caused my mother to be driven by chauffeur up to Oxford, to march into my college rooms and demand through her tears that I cease receiving instruction and stop consorting, as she put it, with my Roman Catholic friends. This time, however, I gave my mother no such assurance and instead harshly ordered the chauffeur to take my mother home.

The day before I was due to be received into the Catholic Church I received a telegram informing me that my mother had been admitted to a London hospital. Fearing that she might be seriously ill, I obtained permission from the dean of the college to travel to London and visit her. On my arrival the annoyed hospital authorities told me that my mother had insisted on being admitted even though there was nothing wrong with her and that she had simply become hysterical. Saying very little, I accompanied her home and immediately returned to Oxford.

If anyone had told me then that at the age of ninety-one, a year before she died, my mother would become a Catholic, I would not have believed them. Such was my anger at the time at what had happened, I irrationally decided to postpone indefinitely becoming a Catholic and told all my friends that I would have nothing further to do with religion of any kind, since it caused too many problems in my life. I felt caught between my filial duty towards a widowed mother and my longing to become the one thing she hated.

For the next two years I gave up going to church altogether and ceased praying. People with anorexia nervosa may, by refusing to eat, endanger their physical and mental health but because of their condition may not realise this danger; in contrast I, by obstinately refusing to pray, knew full well that I was jeopardising my spiritual life. Instead I drifted, indulged myself and in reality was very unhappy. I was irrationally angry with God, my mother and many of the people around me. I felt as though there was a vacuum at the centre of my life which nothing was able to fill, try as I might to fill it with intense activity, pleasure and indulgence of every kind. I felt deprived of the thing I most wanted, namely to become a Catholic. This I instinctively knew would provide me with direction and purpose. Under the circumstances and not able also ultimately to become a priest as I had hoped, I decided, however, to do what seemed to be the next best thing. I would stay at Oxford a further year after graduating in history and train to become a teacher.

As part of the teacher-training course, we were required to spend a placement of three months at a secondary school of our choice. I chose to go to Haberdashers' Aske's, a well-known independent day school for boys in London with a strong academic reputation. Shortly after I arrived there, the head of the history department fell seriously ill and I found myself having to take his classes. I thoroughly enjoyed the opportunity to teach, especially the challenge involved in teaching bright sixth-formers. I also relished the opportunity to embrace life in London, with all its opportunities for going to the opera, the theatre, museums and art exhibitions, not to mention engaging in a hectic social round. It was for this reason that I then decided to embark upon a different career and one that would allow me to remain permanently in London.

Despite the headmaster of Haberdashers' Aske's offering me a full-time post once I had completed my teacher training, I had decided that instead I would seek a civil service post in the House of Commons. There, I foolishly told myself, I would mingle with all the people who ran the country, both members of the government and opposition. I wanted to be at what I considered was the centre of real action. Instead of prayer I now sought worldly influence. When therefore I returned to Oxford to complete my teacher-training course, I made no attempt to apply for any of the posts available in schools for teaching history the following autumn. Instead, I began preparations to take the top civil service examinations with the aim of obtaining a post as an assistant to the Speaker in the House of Commons. It was now, however, that a bizarre and significant event occurred.

One evening, a former member of my college called Graham Wynn, then working in industry, arrived unannounced in my rooms and suggested that we should go out for a drink. He was more an acquaintance than a friend, but I readily agreed to his suggestion and together we set out for the saloon bar of the Randolph Hotel not far away. Once we arrived there I told him of my plans to obtain a post in the House of Commons, an idea that not only made him splutter over his drink but seemed to fill him with abhorrence. In loud and harsh tones he informed me that within three months I would be utterly bored, that I was making the greatest mistake of my life; and he begged me to change my mind. So strongly did he feel these things that, in retrospect, I realised that he there and then determined to make me see what he called reason.

Firstly he persuaded me to drink more alcohol than was good for me and then, when I was beyond caring, he made me promise that before going to bed that night I would write a letter to the Civil Service abandoning my plan to sit their administrative-grade examinations. Largely to placate him, I agreed to his demands and, when I arrived at my digs utterly inebriated at 2.30 the following morning, I sat down, wrote such a letter and went out and posted it. On awakening later that day, I realised what I had done and had no alternative but to revert to the original plan of becoming a schoolmaster.

Oddly, I never encountered that future captain of industry, who died in 2006, ever again, so never discovered why he had taken so much trouble to get me to change my mind. But he was right, I would have been utterly bored, possibly in less than three months, had I gone to work among politicians. Instead, I acquired a post teaching history at Churcher's College, a minor public school in a country market town in Hampshire called Petersfield, and loved it. Even so, the issue of religion and priesthood would not go away. In fact it reached a climax halfway through my time of teaching, when the school underwent a government inspection.

The man who inspected the teaching of history happened to be a direct descendant of Matthew Arnold, the nineteenth-century poet and critic, who also had worked as an inspector of schools. After several days of observing me teaching history to all ages and classes of boys, he took me aside and offered to give me a reference if I would seek to obtain employment in what he called a better school. At first I was flattered but then put off by the fact that he reduced the head of the history department to tears by brutally criticising his teaching methods and lack of organisation in front of me. I considered his remarks true but conveyed in an unprofessional manner. The upshot was that I decided to stay at the school and not place the head of department in an even more embarrassing position.

Nevertheless I wanted desperately to find some way of expressing my thanks to God at having received a highly commendable report on my teaching. I ran down the hill on which the school was situated, and knocked on the door of the local Catholic priest in order to ask him if I could become a Catholic. The door was opened by a balding, rotund priest wearing spectacles and a dog collar, resembling no one so much as the character Father Brown in the G.K. Chesterton detective stories. When I made my request he simply responded by saying yes in the most matter-of-fact way and made an arrangement on the spot for me to begin what is known as instruction in the Catholic faith, with a view to my becoming a Catholic three months later. Little did I know that my life was soon to be radically changed.

The priest in question happened to be a remarkable man. His name was Henry Clarke. A convert to Catholicism himself, he had – I later learned – the unusual gift of receiving into the Catholic Church either very distinguished people, such as the actor Alec Guinness and the war hero Leonard Cheshire VC, or very difficult people. When informed of this later by various people, I guessed which category I belonged to!

It turned out that Henry Clarke was also a deeply spiritual man and a person of great insight. Widely read and anticipating the changes that the Second Vatican Council would introduce, he was above all a great ecumenist, constantly advising me to bring with me into the Catholic Church all the good that I had acquired in Anglicanism. I could have had no better instructor in the process of becoming a Catholic. As time went on we also became great friends. Looking back it seems to me as though in the beginning I resembled a highly spirited animal that needed taming and putting in the right direction, and Henry Clarke was exactly the man to do it. In subsequent years I was to acknowledge the truth of John Henry Newman's dictum that significant meetings between individuals are never accidental, but providential.

Curiously, however, a few days before I was due to become a Catholic, my mother – who knew nothing of my taking instruction again in the Catholic faith – was taken seriously and genuinely ill and rushed into hospital. As Fr Clarke foresaw at the time, if I postponed my reception into the Catholic faith for a third time I would never become a Catholic. I therefore decided to go ahead and break the news to my mother once she had recovered and was out of hospital. What she had undoubtedly known all along was that, if I became a Catholic, I would then inevitably seek to be a priest and she would never have grandchildren. To be fair she also considered the demands made on Catholics by the Church to be heavy.

On 29th March 1962 I became a Catholic. It had taken me virtually ten long years and three attempts to fulfil this hope. I was now twenty-eight. This was also the year that Pope John XXIII was to convene the Second Vatican Council, a meeting of bishops worldwide that would change the face of Catholicism for ever.

Not long after this and in the course of my teaching at Churcher's College, I also founded and ran a sixth-form society, and invited writers, painters, poets and suchlike people to come as guest speakers. It was during this time that the Anglican Bishop of Woolwich published an unusual bestseller called *Honest to God*, so I invited his secretary to come and talk about the book and why it had been such a success with the general public. In my enthusiasm for the fact that many sixth-formers who had never previously shown any interest in religion were now avidly reading the book, I wrote to the then coadjutor or assistant Catholic Bishop of Portsmouth, Thomas Holland, expressing my delight. To my amazement he replied by return of post ordering me to cease forthwith to discuss its contents with my pupils and offering to see me if I wanted an explanation. I wondered if this was the iron fist in a velvet glove which my mother had attributed to all Catholic bishops.

When I went to see Bishop Holland, he sat me down and gave me the equivalent of a long tutorial on the dangers of allowing my pupils to read *Honest to God*. He told me that if it continued they would subsequently go on to read such Protestant authors as Bonhoeffer and Bultmann and lose all their faith. It did little good to point out that none of those in the sixth form were Catholics and the only one who actively practised his faith was an Anglican, but this was just before the Second Vatican Council opened the windows of the Catholic Church to new ideas.

Fr Henry Clarke had earlier intimated to Bishop Holland that I had a vocation, and the bishop had told him that I could expect to be sent to the Beda College in Rome, a college for late vocations. To my dismay, the bishop now terminated this meeting by informing me that I was not ready to be trained for the priesthood, that he would cancel forthwith the place for me to train at the Beda, and that I would have to wait for at least two more years. This seriously upset me, so in my disappointment, and thinking that I had little left to lose, I had the temerity to ask the bishop if the Church would ever reconsider its mind on birth control. (This was in the days before Pope Paul VI set up a commission to investigate the matter.) His voice shook as he gave a resounding "No". Fr Clarke was equally furious with me, but for a different reason. He considered I had been naive.

3

Spiritual direction

A few weeks after this disappointing encounter with the bishop, I had reason to visit my old tutor in history at Oxford. I told him what had occurred in my encounter with Bishop Holland and how disappointed I was at being told that I had to wait two years before beginning to train for the priesthood. He immediately suggested that I return to Oxford the following October, obtain a doctorate in history, and do some teaching at my old college while waiting to enter a seminary. I took up his suggestion and in 1964 returned to Oxford, a somewhat chastened and certainly changed person from when I had left it six years previously. This time I was a Catholic and determined to drown my sorrow in hard work.

The Catholic chaplain to the university at that time was Fr Michael Hollings. He was a giant in every sense of the word. When I first met him he was tall, with black hair carefully parted, the owner of a distinctly long nose and a small, mobile mouth. On his mother's side he was a Dalrymple and related to the Welds, a recusant family among whose members had been a cardinal. A former Guards officer, Michael had been decorated in the Second World War for bravery, but he was also a philanthropist, a writer and an all-round inspirational figure. Most of all he was a man of prayer. Few who met him were left unaltered. To meet him was akin to encountering a huge breath of fresh air.

It was also now that I began consciously to realise how deep an impression a Catholic priest could make on others by the sheer seriousness with which he might take his vocation. No matter how frequently one met Michael, there was always an element within him that defied description and left one with more questions than answers. Almost inevitably I was made to wonder as to the nature of his relationship with God and how, precisely, Michael prayed. How could one be so dedicated, so given over to the service of others, so convinced and committed to Christ?

There were times when he aggravated and infuriated me, not least when he gave orders like a commanding officer, but more than anyone else he inspired me to offer myself for the priesthood. If you had told me then that one day I would occupy his position as Catholic chaplain to Oxford University, I would have been amazed, so highly did I rate him.

During the Second World War Michael had served in the Middle East and Italy, and lost his faith. A meeting with Padre Pio helped him recover it and set him on the path to becoming an exceptional priest. At Oxford he operated an open-door policy at the chaplaincy, turning no caller away and being available to students at all hours of the day and night. His generosity towards those in need was proverbial, leading him on one occasion to hand his bedroom over to a homeless student and thereafter always to sleep on a sofa in his sitting room. It was Michael that made the huge difference to my three years as a postgraduate student at Oxford from 1964 to 1967, during which I wrote a thesis on the intellectual development of Edward Bouverie Pusey, one of the leaders alongside John Henry Newman of the Oxford Movement in the nineteenth century. Several years later I turned this thesis into a biography published under the title of *The Young Doctor Pusey*. Had I not encountered Michael Hollings, however, I doubt whether I would have completed my doctoral thesis, let alone have become a priest. He was pivotal to the direction my life took when I turned thirty.

A few weeks into my first term as a postgraduate a conversation developed among a group of students concerning spiritual direction. As I had not long been a Catholic I had never heard the expression and enquired what it meant. All faces turned to me with astonishment and one of my newly acquired friends said, "But you have one of the finest spiritual directors, if not *the* finest, in the country!" "Who is that?"

I asked. "Michael Hollings, of course," came the reply. Hitherto I had thought of Michael simply as a remarkable and unusual friend, but when it was explained to me what spiritual direction meant, namely being guided and instructed in the different ways to draw close to God through prayer, I thought it sufficiently important to ask Michael to become my director. It turned out to be the most important decision I made at that time and one that had a lasting effect.

If I had ever thought spiritual direction would be an easy option, I was to be proven utterly wrong. Initially at a weekly session, later to become monthly, three-monthly, six-monthly and ultimately on request, Michael taught me how to pray along the lines advocated in the medieval classic *The Cloud of Unknowing*. While never neglecting oral, petitionary, communal, or liturgical prayer, I was masterfully led along the way of the *hesychasts*. In other words I was trained to find, approach and pray to God by eschewing the use of images and words. Michael's aim was to have me understand that – in the words of Simone Weil – "Absolutely unmixed attention is prayer."

In order to achieve this, Michael encouraged me to explore Eastern Orthodox spirituality, particularly the writings of such nineteenth-century Russian saints as Seraphim of Sarov, but most of all *The Way of a Pilgrim*, the work of an anonymous writer, in order to acquaint myself with the Jesus prayer: "Lord Jesus Christ, Son of God, have mercy on me, a sinner."

Michael went on to encourage me to use this prayer, usually slowly and unpacking the meaning of the words as I was uttering them, wherever I happened to be and whenever I had a free moment, such as walking from place to place, waiting for a bus, standing in a queue, or waiting to be served in a restaurant and so on. In time "homing in on God" and giving him my attention at every available moment became almost automatic (I called it going into orbit), and it became, as St Catherine of Siena once said, like carrying a monastic cell around within one.

Combined with regular all-night vigils before the Blessed Sacrament in the chaplaincy chapel, attendance at daily Mass, regular retreats and constant reading of the scriptures or spiritual writers, Michael trained me as though I were one of his recruits in a Guards regiment. For three years there was no let-up, so much so that Henry Clarke became alarmed and made a special visit to Oxford to satisfy himself that Michael was not overdoing things. He went away, however, not only reassured but amazed at my happiness at discovering this thing called contemplative prayer. At that time I was only in what I termed the foothills of prayer, with all the different consolations usually showered by God on a newcomer. It was only later that I realised that I was just one of Michael's many apprentices, and beyond the excitements, the satisfactions and joys of a person starting to pray in the foothills, there lay the equivalent of huge mountains to scale and particular temptations to face – for the rest of my life. Nevertheless I have never had any regrets about the way Michael Hollings taught me to encounter God in prayer. It radically changed my life for good.

The second major difference Michael made to my life occurred as a result of his literally ordering me to join the Oxford students' annual pilgrimage to Lourdes and work among those who were sick. I told him that Lourdes and the kind of devotions to Mary found there were not my cup of tea, but he wouldn't listen. I told him that I had only £17 in the bank so could not afford to go to Lourdes, whereupon he informed me that he had already paid for my ferry and train ticket there. In fact all my protestations were in vain, so in July 1965 I found myself on board a ferry bound for Calais and then on a train for Paris and Lourdes.

On the train from Paris we didn't even have couchettes, but sat up all night in packed compartments, arriving at Lourdes the following morning utterly tired, bleary-eyed and grumpy. Then we made our way to our bunk-bed accommodation in dormitories at a youth hostel, called the Abri Saint-Michel, where we were fed on a basic diet of coffee, soup, potatoes and beans, before beginning a daily routine of washing, clothing and tending the sick pilgrims housed in two hospitals.

After giving the sick pilgrims their breakfast we pushed them in wheelchairs or carried them on stretchers to be bathed in the spring water or to the grotto for Mass where St Bernadette had seen her visions of Mary, and after lunch in the afternoons we lined up the sick pilgrims for a blessing from the various bishops and prelates holding up the Blessed Sacrament before them. In the evening all the helpers and pilgrims took part in a torchlight procession. This became our daily routine for the next seven days, beginning at seven in the morning and carrying on until nine or ten at night, with breaks for hurried meals in the youth hostel.

At first I was bombarded with a variety of conflicting emotions. I was horrified at the rampant commercialism of the town, but could not but admire the peace and quiet of the large area called the Domain, the place where the hospitals, major churches and grotto were located and where all the religious activities took place, especially the celebration of the Mass. I was soon physically exhausted by both the hard work and the long hours involved in attending to the needs of the sick pilgrims, but completely dumbstruck by the patience and indeed happiness of those who were sick, many of whom were suffering all manner of incurable illnesses. Their devotion to Mary, the Mother of God, made me ashamed of my reluctance to come to Lourdes in the first place. I envied them their faith.

In view of this I returned to Oxford seriously changed in yet another way from how I had been a year previously. Unexpectedly I had also encountered at Lourdes an Italian medical student called Gianpaolo Donzelli, who later on would make a great difference to my life, but at the time I did not know this. Awaiting my return was also a letter from the secretary of Harold Wilson, the Prime Minister, informing me that I would be receiving a grant to cover the cost of my final year of postgraduate studies, so my financial problems were solved. So great was the effect on me of Lourdes that after that I went on pilgrimage there more times than I can now remember.

One of my most valued friends during these postgraduate years at Oxford was a young, attractive and highly intelligent woman, with a constantly enquiring mind and an infectious sense of humour, called Peggy. I was extremely fond of Peggy, but by now my heart was truly set on becoming a priest. Years later Peggy would become a well-known eye consultant and Fellow of New College. She also married a hugely talented and immensely dedicated master at the Dragon Preparatory School in Oxford, called Robin Frith, and they had two sons. To my immense joy, Peggy also later converted to Catholicism.

Towards the end of my three years as a postgraduate I completed my doctoral thesis and was invited to meet the new Bishop of Portsmouth, Derek Worlock. (Providentially, some months previously, Thomas Holland, the bishop who had told me I was not ready to become a priest, had been translated to a diocese in the north of England.) On this occasion Bishop Worlock was accompanied by his secretary, a tall, lanky and charming priest, called Cormac Murphy-O'Connor, who would later become well known himself and indeed succeed Cardinal Hume as the Archbishop of Westminster.

To my astonishment Bishop Worlock asked where I would like to train as a priest. This was a quite different approach from that of Bishop Holland and was the beginning of a relationship that was never easy, and at times full of difficulties, but one from which I learnt a great deal and which lasted without a break until his death in 1996.

Derek Worlock was a bishop fully imbued with the spirit of the Second Vatican Council, which he had attended as a *peritus* or expert and adviser to the English and Welsh bishops. Before coming to the Portsmouth diocese he had been the private secretary to at least three cardinals at Westminster and no one knew the inner workings of the Church better than he. He was also a gifted networker and brilliant committee man. His chief flaws, however, could be perceived as his craving the limelight – woe betide anyone who upstaged him – and a hunger for acceptance. Although his manner may have appeared stiff and outwardly cold, these were attributes that belied the warm and often generous nature beneath. Despite his very human failings and the fact that we did not always see eye to eye, I count myself extremely fortunate to have had him as my bishop.

In answer to Bishop Worlock's question about where I would like to be trained as a priest I replied that most of all I would like to study under the leading English Catholic theologian of the time, Fr Charles Davis. Bishop Worlock said that he and Davis had been at seminary together, were friends and he would arrange it. Two months later, however, Charles Davis announced he was leaving the Catholic Church and priesthood, got married and soon after emigrated to Canada. This was a massive shock to the Catholic Church in England and yet again it seemed that my progress towards priesthood would be delayed.

It was then, however, that I received a letter from Bishop Worlock saying that, in view of what had happened, he had provisionally booked me a place at the English College in Rome to study for the priesthood and he wanted to know if I wished to take up the place. I consulted Michael Hollings and together we agreed that I should go to Rome the following September. Little did I know that I was about to begin probably the five most formative years of my life.

4

The English College, Rome

The Venerable English College in Rome, or the *Venerabile* to its alumni, began its existence in the Middle Ages as a hospice for English pilgrims, later it became the property of the English Crown and, after the Reformation, it became a seminary. At one time regarded as the Sandhurst for the Catholic Church in England because of the number of its students who became bishops, it was also the place where its future priests acquired a unique Roman manner and style.

To be trained and educated in Rome was the dream of many students for the priesthood, not only from England but from countries all around the world. Its obvious asset was that it gave one an opportunity to become aware of the international and universal dimension of the Church, with every major country in the world having its own college or seminary in Rome and its students attending one of the many different ecclesiastical universities scattered around the city. Every day a student for the priesthood mingled with others from such diverse places as North and South America, India, Germany, France, Africa, the Far East and so on, against a backdrop of ancient buildings, churches and landmarks renowned either for their beauty or for their historical importance. The different liturgical seasons in the life of the Church too, which were celebrated throughout the city, especially those of Advent, Christmas, Lent and Easter, were to leave an indelible mark in the minds of future Roman-trained priests.

In 1967, when I arrived in Rome at the age of thirty-three, there was no shortage of vocations for the priesthood and at the English College at that time we numbered seventy. Rather like at the universities of Oxford and Cambridge it was the college that left the deepest impression on a student; but in this case, because the seventy of us were thrown together in a foreign country and only infrequently went home to England, the impact we made on each other was greater. The atmosphere of the college was one that fostered lasting, often lifelong, friendships among its students.

Whereas I quickly had deep reservations about and became impatient with the continental method of teaching at the university that English students attended – the Jesuit-run Pontifical Gregorian University – with its emphasis on lectures and repeating information from lectures in examinations, I knew from the start that the communal nature of the college was where I would most be moulded and shaped for priesthood. It was impossible not to be so when one lived side by side with others aiming for the same goal, sharing the same lifestyle, eating together, spending one's leisure time together, and most of all praying and attending Mass together every day for five or six years, sometimes seven.

Like all seminaries the world over, the English College in Rome had yet to experience the full force of the changes inaugurated by the Second Vatican Council in the way priests were trained. The Council had ended only two years previously and for my first year the system of training and the way the college functioned were as they had been for decades.

Each day we rose at 5.30 a.m. in order to be in chapel at 6 a.m. for half an hour of what was called Meditation. During this time we were encouraged either to read a spiritual book, on a subject such as the life of one of the saints or some aspect of Christ's teaching, or to consider some episode of Christ's life. Meditation was not strictly speaking prayer itself but an aid to prayer.

At 6.30 a.m. we recited morning prayer together and attended community Mass, followed by breakfast at 7.30 a.m. At 8.15 a.m. we gathered in crocodile formation to walk together to the university for four forty-minute lectures in Latin. We were usually dressed in clerical garb, with students from the different colleges wearing cassocks or soutanes of different colours or waistbands, making their way in colourful processions through the streets of Rome.

At 12.45p.m. we returned to the college in the same manner for lunch, after which we made brief prayers of thanksgiving in the chapel and then went to our rooms for a siesta until 4 p.m. The following two hours were our own and then we either studied in our rooms or had tutorials from a member of the college staff, followed by evening prayer all together in the chapel and then supper at 8.15 p.m. (Meals were provided by a community of nuns and the weekly cleaning of our rooms was done by a group of usually married Italian working-class women.)

After supper we gathered in the college common room for a quaint custom called Circles. This name derived from the fact that all of us sat in circles each of about ten students and were encouraged to make conversation with each other. The idea was to enable us to become socialised but, so that "particular friendships" should not be formed, we were not permitted to sit in the same circle on consecutive evenings. (Similarly when out walking we were discouraged from doing so in pairs.)

At the end of Circles we went to the chapel for the final prayer of the day, called Compline, after which we retired for the night at 10 p.m. and then began what was known as the Great Silence. We were not permitted to leave our rooms, visit friends, or engage in conversations until the following morning.

This routine occurred every weekday, except on a Thursday, which was regarded as a free day – free of university lectures and a day for *gita* or time for exploring the sights of Rome and the surrounding countryside. Groups of students invariably went off to the Alban Hills and the college villa, bordering Lake Albano and opposite the papal summer palace of Castel Gandolfo. (It was at the villa that the majority of students lived during the summer months of June to September.) On Thursdays we were required to be back in college by 10 p.m. On Sundays we celebrated a more formal type of Mass with music, often with English visitors to Rome in attendance, after which we might find ourselves acting as their guides around the various churches and shrines of the city.

At Christmas we put on a serious play and a pantomime for the English residents living in Rome, but we were discouraged from visiting private homes or making friends among Italians living in the city. Altogether we were a small, essentially English-speaking community, inward-looking and shielded from any of the happenings outside the college walls, except those related to ecclesiastical ceremonies at the great basilicas around the city. (In 1968 during the time of student riots in Rome and other major cities throughout Europe, we were confined to the college and indeed locked in and forbidden to go outside.) Inevitably therefore we were thrown together in what felt like a hermetically sealed bubble, with only each other to rely upon. For those who lasted the course to ordination, the end result was that they formed deep and lasting friendships for the rest of their lives.

The staff of the college consisted of a rector whom all students addressed as Sir; a vice-rector, essentially responsible for discipline and finance; a spiritual director to oversee our prayer lives and to give us weekly spiritual talks; and a philosophy tutor to assist us to comprehend what our Jesuit masters were teaching us at the university.

During the greater part of my time at the college the rector was a saintly monsignor called Leo Alston from Liverpool. He was an eminent classical scholar and a man of immense kindness; at the same time, largely because of a somewhat timid and sometimes stubborn nature, he disliked intensely having to take decisions, was at the mercy of more powerful personalities and was occasionally bullied by bishops.

The vice-rector of the college, Jack Brewer, who subsequently became Bishop of Lancaster, was a strong-willed and strong-minded man and, like myself, a redhead. He was the type of person with whom, paradoxically, it was necessary first to have a fight before one could be friends with him. Then he was a loyal and fierce friend and a man with a big heart.

I discovered his strong will one summer, when I was due to travel to England to visit my octogenarian mother. When I asked him if I could extend my stay by just twenty-four hours, in order to attend in Newcastle the ordination to the priesthood of a fellow student and close friend, Tony Battle, he was adamant in his refusal.

"Oh, no, David, you cannot have an extension even for twenty-four hours because your place is here with your community," he told me.

"But I'm only asking for one more day," I answered.

"No, David, your place is with your community."

"But we only get ordained once in our lives, just as we only get baptised once and those who marry hopefully only experience marriage once, so if I don't get to Tony's ordination this time, I never shall."

Again he repeated that nevertheless my place was with the college community in Rome. At this point, seeing that he would never give me permission, I thought I had little to lose by speaking my mind and telling him something that few other people knew.

"You know why you are refusing me permission?" I shouted at him.

"Yes," he said and yet again repeated his reason.

"No," I said through gritted teeth. "The reason is something else. When you were a student at the seminary you were very fond of your sister. She was suddenly taken seriously ill and you were not informed. She died and you were not informed. You were not even allowed to attend her funeral. Only afterwards were you told that she had been ill and died."

"Of course," I continued, "this was in the old days when it was thought that becoming a priest meant leaving family and friends behind one, but that is the heartless treatment you were given and why you are giving it to me."

"Oh, David," said Jack, "how can you say that?"

"Because it's true," I answered.

We ended our meeting by him saying, "David, I have learnt a lot this morning."

"You haven't learnt a bloody thing," I retorted, before storming out of his office and slamming the door.

I never did get to Tony Battle's ordination, but after our fight Jack Brewer treated me quite differently and in later years as a good friend. This was so much so that, several years later, when he spotted me at a meeting of the Catholic hierarchy at which I was required to be in attendance, he pushed his way through the throng of prelates, gave me a massive hug and welcomed me with open arms.

The spiritual director, Tom Curtis-Hayward, was quite different, a bundle of contradictions and fascinated by psychology – someone to avoid unless one was prepared to become a guinea pig in his latest pseudo-scientific attempt to explain human nature. Because I refused to participate in his activities and sought instead spiritual direction from a remarkable American Jesuit called Don Hinfey, based outside the college, Tom once wrote me a letter in which he described me the most obstinate student he had ever encountered. I enquired of the rector whether I had his permission to reply to this, at which the rector smiled broadly and genially replied that it might do some good.

Tom, a gifted man in many ways, did not last long at the college and was subsequently recalled to pastoral duties back home in England. Before leaving Rome, however, and despite our differences, Tom was magnanimous enough to take me aside and counsel me to persevere at the college, because he believed I was truly being called to be a priest.

The philosophy tutor, Christopher Budd, was a product himself of the college, tall and, like many tall people, very humble; and someone with whom I had been friends at Oxford. Indeed, Michael Hollings, my spiritual director at Oxford, used to call us Eeyore and Piglet whenever he encountered us walking together! Later Christopher was to become the rector of Wonersh seminary near Guildford and afterwards the Bishop of Plymouth. He was the epitome of moderation in his opinions, a person who heartily disliked controversy and who accepted without murmuring whatever the hand of fortune dealt him. He remains a good friend to this day.

Without a doubt, however, it was the influence that students had on one another, especially those to whom one naturally gravitated, that left its mark on each of us. This was particularly the case after my first year when the changes brought about by the Second Vatican Council finally hit the college with full force. The result was that the daily routine was virtually abandoned, Italian took the place of Latin at the university, clerical garb was worn less often by students, and a generally more lax tone emanated throughout the college. Increasingly the effect students had on one another took the place of that of the staff.

In my case I was greatly influenced by the fourteen students in my own year, more than a few of whom would go on to occupy significant positions in the Church. This was particularly so of one called Philip Carroll from Newcastle, who won my friendship because even then he was capable of uttering considerable wisdom in down-to-earth terms. In years to come he would become the spiritual director of the college.

The example of a handful of students higher up in the college, however, made an even deeper impression on me. Among them were three in particular, namely a future Archbishop of Westminster, Vincent Nichols, who hailed from Liverpool, radiated charm and good humour, and whose no-nonsense father had more than once advised him never to refuse any office that came his way in the Church and never to ask for one; John Guest, a talented and highly intelligent young man from the diocese of Nottingham, who retained his individuality through thick and thin; and, above all, a brilliant and deeply committed left-wing radical, called Tony Battle, whose ordination I had sought to attend.

Tony, a graduate of London University, hailed from Washington, County Durham, and was no mean theologian. It was debatable as to which predominated in his make-up – his intellectual ability or his highly sensitive nature, which was utterly empathetic to those who were poor, outcast and oppressed. His chief obvious asset, however, was his refusal to have any truck with hypocrisy, humbug or pretence. His discipleship of Christ – not achieved without a struggle – was second to none. Unknown to most people, once a week he used to take me with him to visit the poor people of the city, giving them food bought out of his own money and doing various jobs for them. In so many ways he and I were opposites, but what he taught me during my seminary days, and during the subsequent nearly forty years before his premature death, is incalculable. This was particularly true of the many occasions when I clashed with the authorities and sometimes openly disregarded college rules.

An event I particularly remember, and which amused Tony, occurred on the occasion of my thirty-fifth birthday. On the morning in question I went to the rector's office and, after greeting me kindly but with a slightly apprehensive look, as though he was wondering what I wanted, he enquired how he could help me.

"Well," I began, "I am thirty-five today and I was wondering if you consider me old enough to have a key to the college."

"Oh, dear," he replied. "This is entirely unprecedented."

"Yes, I realise that," I responded. (He could tell from my stance, however, that I would wait as long as it took for him to come to a decision.)

"Oh, dear, oh dear," he said. "I suppose so." His voice trailed off, with him clearly worried about what this would entail. He then reached into a drawer of his desk, took out a key to the side door of the college and handed it to me.

"Thank you very much indeed," I said, truly grateful and thinking I had actually made a small dent in the four-hundred-year-old history of the college.

Alas, it was also one of the worst things I ever did. Once the news spread among the other students that I had a key, scarcely a night passed without me being disturbed by shouts up to my window, which looked on to the street below, from students locked out but not worried because they knew I had a key. "Dave," they would shout, "throw down the key, please."

Wearily I would climb out of bed, insert the key in a glove and throw it down into the street. It was astonishing how many gloves I wore out during the next three years. Today all the students have keys to the college.

College rules especially infuriated me when they concerned relations with the outside world. From the outset I made a conscious decision to disregard the rule that forbade us to enter private houses, not least because my friend Piero Bozzetti, whom I had first met in Paris thirteen years previously, had a house in Rome. There were times when visits to his house took on the aspect of a refuge for me from all things claustrophobic about the college, including things ecclesiastical. It was he who also made me aware of Italian culture and of the wider world outside the bounds of church life. Our friendship became closer when

I donated blood on his behalf on one occasion when he was suddenly taken ill and required an operation. Because I gave blood for him so unhesitatingly, his mother declared that, from then on, I was to think of myself as a member of their family. There was no way after that that I would abide by any college rule forbidding me to enter any Italian private house!

Similarly, soon after arriving in Rome I had renewed my friendship with the Italian medical student I had first met in Lourdes two years previously, called Gianpaolo Donzelli. He invited me to holiday at his home in Rovigo near Padua during vacation times and on one memorable occasion drove me in a blizzard to my brother's grave high in the Apennine Mountains. After I had cleared the snow from the grave of this brother of mine, who had been killed in the Second World War, and after saying some prayers, Gianpaolo declared that henceforth he would be my brother. Initially I took this simply as a kind and typical Italian gesture, but only later, when he announced his decision to every member of his family and to all his friends, did I realise that he was serious. Even today, years later, when he is a distinguished paediatrician living in Florence, with a daughter who is a doctor, he continues to regard me as his brother. It was from Gianpaolo's home during holidays from the college that I visited such Italian cities as Venice, Verona, Padua, Florence, Siena and Assisi, and deepened my love of all things Italian.

Another private house that I frequented was that of a Jewish family living in Trastevere, the oldest and most fascinating part of Rome. I had become acquainted with this particular family when they came to a college production one Christmas of the play *Hadrian the Seventh*, in which I had played the part of the Pope. At their home I imbibed Jewish customs and beliefs, became acquainted with people involved in the arts, politics and business, and began taking a great interest in all things to do with Israel. Soon I also decided to apply for a summer travel scholarship to Israel, using my time at military school, my two years' national service, and my father's and brother's military background as an opportunity to obtain the scholarship. I succeeded and in the summer of

1969 spent three months in Israel studying, unusually for a future priest, the training methods of the Israeli army. For part of the time in this visit to the Holy Land I was accompanied by Vincent Nichols, whose parents and brothers I had got to know at their home in Liverpool.

This was a time of ebullient optimism in Israel, a period when perhaps the majority at least of young Israelis considered that a negotiated lasting peace was attainable with the Arabs. The experience therefore of living and working side by side in army barracks and on manoeuvres with Israeli recruits of both sexes, listening to their hopes and fears, and observing how Jewish immigrants from all over the world were determined to carve out a future for themselves, was an extraordinary and uplifting experience. It was only towards the end of my stay, when I once asked the blunt question of a high authority as to whether Israelis truly wanted peace with the Arabs, and was told that, in the event of lasting peace occurring, then divisions among the different sections of Israeli society would surface, that I began to qualify my attitude to this amazing country.

I combined my researches with the army in 1969 with visits to many of the holy places mentioned in the Bible. Then, before leaving Israel, I was offered a job teaching history at the University of Haifa. Attractive though the offer was, I pointed out that I still wanted to be a priest, and was then bluntly informed that if I accepted the offer I would be so busy trying to stay alive that I wouldn't have time to think about my soul. This was a time when Israel was completely surrounded by nations, including Egypt, hostile to its existence, so the comment was nothing if not practical.

Among the businessmen I encountered at the home of my Jewish friends in Rome was an American called Burt Fagan. Inevitably, given the influence on me of Tony Battle's left-wing views, Burt and I clashed loudly on the matter of American capitalism and what I termed his responsibility to consider the plight of the world's poor rather than feathering his own nest. One day, however, our verbal battles turned into an unexpected and extended truce.

At supper one evening in an Italian restaurant, an Anglo-Irish colleague of Burt's began berating John Guest, a fellow student and good friend of mine, for being what he called "unproductive", on account of the fact that as a future priest John was required, like myself, to be celibate. John, who was not only reserved but exceedingly polite, refused to defend himself, whereas there was no way that I could stand idly by and watch him being insulted. Within minutes I told the Anglo-Irishman to cease attacking my friend and, for good measure, I also told him to remove his hand from the knee of the woman sitting next to him, who happened to be someone else's wife.

The Anglo-Irishman was understandably angry at being caught out and he immediately challenged me to accompany him outside to settle the matter with fisticuffs! It was then that Burt, a large bear of a man, stood up and declared that anyone threatening me would have him to deal with him – an attitude for which I was immensely grateful. The Anglo-Irishman, realising he had met more than his match, sank back immediately into his seat.

I was naturally indebted to Burt, who informed me that, in order to repay his kindness, I had no option but to visit America and investigate at his expense American capitalism and the American way of life for myself. This I did the following summer, researching among other things racism, drug addiction and inner-city problems in New York, Washington and Boston.

As a child Burt had been sent by his mother every Sunday to catechism classes and Mass, with a dime in his pocket for the collection, with all the other children in the neighbourhood. One Sunday Burt had the temerity to question what one of the nuns giving the catechism class was teaching. Her response was to send for the parish priest, who clipped Burt's ear and ordered him out of the church. Burt never again went either to catechism classes or to Mass, but instead went each Sunday to the local railway station and spent the dime his mother had given him on back numbers of the *Wall Street Journal*. His mother never knew.

As Burt lay on his deathbed years later, having suffered a massive stroke, I informed him that, as he was soon to die, as a priest I wanted his soul back for God. He looked me straight in the eye and said that I had had his soul in my keeping for years.

One of the most puzzling questions for me at the English College was why the seventy different young men there had offered themselves for the priesthood. When I concluded that this student wanted to be a priest because his mother had wished it, that one because he was frightened of sex, this one because he actually wanted to be an actor but hadn't the courage to enter the precarious life offered in the theatre and so on, I inevitably wondered why I had offered myself. In other words, though I was convinced that God was calling me to be a priest, I started to ask myself what were the worldly reasons for my decision.

Among the memorable people I had met at the home of the Jewish family in Rome, with whom I spent much of my free time, was the mother of the family, an accomplished pianist who was also a devotee of the works of the psychoanalyst Sigmund Freud and his disciples. In order to show her devotion to the Master, she had caused a massive portrait of him to be hung in the downstairs lavatory of the house, to ensure that no one forgot him at critical times in the day. Given her virtually professional knowledge of Freud's ideas, I asked her to assist me to discover the ordinary human reasons why I wanted to become a priest. For the next three years, therefore, I was in a sense peeled like an onion. This was highly instructive, at times unnerving and invariably exhausting, but at the end I considered that I had learnt not only all the significant aspects of my make-up, but the ordinary reasons why I wanted to be a priest. These latter consisted of such things as a love of preaching the word, a desire to introduce others to the significance of the Gospel and – influenced by Tony Battle – a massive desire to assist people in need and poverty.

There was, however, an area of my life that defied analysis. This was the spiritual side of my life, without which I knew I would be unable ever to be fully alive. Whereas this bewildered my Jewish friend, it delighted me. It confirmed for me that the experience I had had as child on a beach in north Devon, and which I wrote of earlier, was authentic. I was thrilled that three years of being peeled had revealed that deep down I was being called to be a priest by God.

Almost inevitably after this, I arranged to undergo privately the *Spiritual Exercises* of St Ignatius of Loyola under the supervision of an expert Jesuit. As I suspected, this enabled me to penetrate deeply that area of my life which had defied analysis – an area which previously only Michael Hollings at Oxford had opened up to me. However, this experience of the *Exercises*, although extremely valuable, convinced me that Ignatian spirituality was not for me. I much preferred and would continue always to prefer the writings of the medieval English school of mystics.

In the summer of my penultimate year at the college I was ordained a deacon alongside the fourteen other members of my year. This took place at Palazzola, the amazingly beautiful college villa, looking down on Lake Albano. At one point in the ceremony a candidate places his hands in those of the ordaining bishop and solemnly swears to obey his own bishop and his lawful successors. When it was my turn, instead of answering immediately, I took my time to consider the implications of this, causing the ordaining bishop to be concerned, squeeze my hands and urgently whisper that I should be responding.

Later that summer, now that we were deacons, all the members of my year were sent to England for a couple of months to acquire pastoral experience in parishes. I was sent to a parish in the town of Basingstoke in Hampshire, lately enlarged to accommodate a massive number of huge housing estates. There I was to be supervised by an extremely able parish priest and former English College man, called Brian Scantlebury, who died in 2008.

For me at least Brian Scantlebury became almost a father figure. He was someone I could respect for being astonishingly hard-working, a person of integrity, a resolute ecumenist and someone who was passionate in his desire to bring Christ's message to the people of Basingstoke, many of whom were from London and were having problems adjusting to life on the housing estates newly built for them. It seemed to me that he was ideally suited both as a person and as a priest for ministering to those in such a situation. At times in the future he was also someone to whom I would turn for sound advice and considerable common sense.

Nevertheless Brian could also be a demanding person, with high expectations of those who were sent to work with him. These qualities did not always endear him to his assistants or to some of those people who came his way. Although he invariably endeavoured to adhere strictly to the truth in whatever he said, he sometimes could be abrasive and almost merciless in his criticisms, giving little leeway for the small failings of others. I realised I was observing a perfectionist at work and even in this I tried to learn from the experience. Because I knew I was to be in Basingstoke for a limited period before returning to Rome for my final year, I felt able to extract from this time all that was useful and valuable, and overlook those things that, over a long period, would probably have been intolerable.

Under the circumstances I remained forever grateful to Brian for first introducing me to such basic experiences as what it meant to live cheek by jowl with priest colleagues in a presbytery, how important it was not to differentiate in the amount of attention and care one gave to the different people in a parish no matter one's personal feelings, how to share the joy of parents at the baptism of their newly born children, how to walk alongside parishioners grieving the loss of loved ones, and even how necessary it was to keep on top of the more mundane activities associated with administration in a parish.

At the end of this period of pastoral training and towards the end of my five years in Rome I was informed that I was being considered as a candidate to enter what is called the Accademia, the institution for the training of Vatican diplomats, based near the Pantheon. Part of me was attracted to the idea of such a prospect, but ultimately nothing came of it and in retrospect this was all for the good.

Before studying in Rome I had often listened to the advice of a man whom I called my godfather and who had encouraged me to become a priest. He was Archbishop Eugene Cardinale, one-time Apostolic Delegate to Great Britain and later Papal Nuncio to Belgium and Luxembourg. My friendship with Archbishop Cardinale had given me the opportunity to observe at first hand the daily life of a diplomat and instinctively I knew that it was not the life for me. In my heart of hearts

I knew that diplomacy was neither my strong point nor my vocation, not least because it was usually divorced from the lives of the ordinary men and women whom I felt called to serve as a priest.

I left Rome for England for the last time at the end of my training in June 1972. I was sad to leave a city that now had many memories for me, but I looked forward eagerly to beginning priestly work in England.

5

Parish life

During my period at the English College it was the custom to be ordained to the priesthood some time during one's final year. Some students were ordained in Rome, others in their home dioceses in England. I was ordained on 25th March 1972, the feast of the Annunciation, in St John's Cathedral, Portsmouth.

The week before one was ordained was traditionally spent in retreat. This was a time of prayer and reflection in preparation for the event that one had spent years previously training for and looking forward to. I spent the week at Quarr, the Benedictine abbey on the Isle of Wight. It was my first visit ever to Quarr and at that time little did I know that within the community of monks was one in particular – a future abbot – whose life would become entwined with mine in an important way, both of us influencing each other.

At the end of my retreat I took the ferry to Portsmouth in order to spend the final night, before ordination to the priesthood, under the roof of Bishop Derek Worlock. This was the usual custom of Portsmouth candidates for the priesthood, as was that of being sent for by the bishop at 8 p.m. and being asked by him whether one had any problems in the face of becoming a priest. We all knew this to be the custom and, almost invariably and accurately, most people replied that ordination was what they had looked forward to for years and that they knew of no problems to prevent it. I, however, was different.

Making my way to the bishop's house from the ferry earlier in the day, I had passed a clergyman who gave the appearance of a thin desiccated stick; his face was like parchment covered in wrinkles, and he looked as one who had had his life drained of all human emotion. The sight had left a deep impression on me. When the bishop asked me whether I had any problems about ordination, doubtless much to his exasperation (after all, I had not ever been a docile student for the priesthood), I told him of my fear that, largely as a result of celibacy, priesthood would one day leave me as dry as a stick and drained of emotion. Much to my relief he gently informed me that that would never be my problem! The following day in the Cathedral of St John he ordained me at long last a priest at the age of thirty-eight.

Present at my ordination were my mother; my Aunt Ethel, from Derby; my Jewish Indian aunt, Sally; Tony Battle; Vincent Nichols; Michael Hollings from Oxford, and Henry Clarke, who had received me into the Catholic Church – in other words, all those who had played a significant part one way or another in my ultimately receiving the sacrament of ordination, which, according to Catholic teaching, leaves an irrevocable and indelible mark on one. Even today, decades later, I can still recall the absolute joy I felt that day, regarding it as the culmination of so many hopes and dreams since that day on the beach in north Devon when I was aged nine.

To my embarrassment but also my amazement and delight, at the reception that followed the ceremony my mother upstaged Bishop Worlock by jumping out of her seat, interrupting him and publicly announcing that this was the happiest day of her life. Everyone applauded.

The following September, Bishop Worlock informed me that I was to begin my priestly ministry by becoming the second curate in the inner-city parish of St Edmund in Southampton. It is the experience of most young priests that they never forget the first parish to which they are assigned. Even now, more than three decades later, the names of the people and the streets of St Edmund's are bright in my memory, whereas those of later parishes either fade or merge with others in my mind. Furthermore, I was never to be so happy again in parish work as I was there, wrongly believing that this was to be the pattern of my daily life for the rest of my life.

St Edmund's in 1972 was an extensive parish at the centre of a large and busy seaport. It included a hospital, two convents, two Catholic schools – one primary and one secondary – and the red-light area. My daily life consisted of saying Mass for the nuns at a nearby convent every weekday morning at 7.15, spending the greater part of the rest of the morning at the large comprehensive girls' school where I was the school chaplain, and after lunch systematically knocking on doors and visiting parishioners in their homes, welcoming newcomers to the parish, taking Holy Communion to housebound elderly and sick people, or conducting funerals. In the evenings before supper, the hours were spent preparing young couples for marriage, instructing converts to Catholicism in the rudiments of the faith, or counselling parishioners who had problems. On Saturdays my fellow curate and I heard confessions in the morning and evening for two and a half hours and, in those days, there were usually queues of people – many coming from distant parts of the city – waiting to be shriven. On Saturday afternoons usually either at Easter or in the summer there were weddings at which to officiate. On Sundays we said several Masses at which we also preached and afterwards administered baptisms.

As the most junior and youngest curate I was given the largest area of the parish as my particular responsibility. This included the colourful and vibrant red-light area, inhabited by pimps, prostitutes and immigrants. The days – apart from Mondays which were by tradition a priest's day off – were usually packed to capacity and fulfilling. For good measure I was also persuaded by the youth officer of the parish to accompany him and lend a hand of an evening to some nuns in the city, known as Sisters of Our Lady of Charity, in their work among adolescent girls in care. These latter were usually Londoners, full of energy and mischief and aching for the bright lights of the capital. In short they were a handful.

Despite the lack of money and occasional frustrations at St Edmund's, I nevertheless felt needed and was never bored. In addition to one's board and lodging, one received a salary of £39 each quarter and, since I could not afford a car, I rode everywhere around the parish on a bicycle.

The parish priest was a highly educated, articulate and true Irish gentleman, ordained before I was born. In those days the diocesan priesthood functioned on a system according to which everything revolved around how many years one had been ordained. As one became more senior, so one was promoted, firstly serving in different parishes as a curate and then eventually becoming a parish priest. Then one was given a larger parish with one assistant, and finally with several. In those days it was the responsibility of a parish priest to guide and supervise the work of his assistants, so I counted myself blessed to have Canon Dwyer as my parish priest. It was well known that some parish priests were severe taskmasters and consequently were given the nickname of "curate bashers". Life for an assistant priest under them was no joke.

It could take several years before one became a parish priest and there was considerable rivalry between priests to obtain the most prestigious parishes. Canon Gerry Dwyer, my first parish priest, was the occupant of what was termed a "plum" parish with two curates, I being the junior.

Apart from conscientiously saying his daily Mass and his prayers, it was well known that Gerry Dwyer did little else except read assiduously from his copious library the latest works on theology as well as the most ancient, combining this with playing golf twice a week. The house or presbytery in which the three of us lived, each with a bedroom and sitting room, was maintained by a scatterbrained Irish housekeeper and cook, truly called Molly Malone, and assisted by a weekly cleaner.

The three of us priests usually only met at mealtimes, but we curates were cross-examined by the Canon at supper time as to what we had done during the day. Often, as I was the newly ordained priest fresh from Rome, he would quiz me on matters to do with philosophy or theology. Whereas my fellow curates heartily disliked this form of inquisition, I actually revelled in it to such an extent that, whereas I observed fellow curates being moved on to other parishes, I continued to remain at St Edmund's, presumably at the Canon's request, for what turned out to be five years.

When Canon Dwyer died some years later, his brother told me that I could take as many of his brother's books as I liked. However, I simply took a small bust of Cardinal Newman which had stood on the mantelpiece in the presbytery dining room and which had witnessed so much of the theological cut and thrust I had had with the Canon.

More than a few could only see Gerry Dwyer's failings and it is true that his particular blind spot was his refusal to part with money, asking me on one celebrated occasion whether I actually needed my £39 quarterly salary. On the other hand, it became a habit with me to point out to his critics that the Second Vatican Council, with all its often sweeping changes, such as ordering the Mass to be celebrated facing the people and in the vernacular, had turned his familiar world upside down and that he and his generation should be regarded with compassion. During my five years at St Edmund's from 1972 to 1977 the Canon and I never once exchanged a harsh word, which was something of a record for me with my red hair, and for which I was grateful.

Another of my duties while I was at St Edmund's was to act as the Catholic representative to the local radio, Radio Solent. Although I enjoyed speaking on the radio I was never convinced that local radio was of any real influence in the lives of its listeners, but it did give me an insight into the workings of the media in general. This was especially so when, early one morning, I received a phone call from Bishop Worlock's secretary telling me to report at once to Bishop's House in Portsmouth and to tell no one, not even the Canon, where I was going.

When I arrived the secretary immediately greeted me with the information that "it's not Westminster", a remark the meaning of which temporarily escaped me. Then I was told that "it's Liverpool", whereupon I realised that the secretary was speaking of Bishop Worlock being promoted to the archbishopric of Liverpool. My instructions were to distribute this information, together with the curriculum vitae and photographs of the bishop, not only to the local radio, but to BBC television stations in the south and all the regional newspapers for release at 11.00 that morning, the same time as the news would be released in Rome. Simultaneously with this news it was to be announced that Basil Hume, the Abbot of Ampleforth, was to become the Archbishop of Westminster, the post that it was thought Bishop Worlock had desired.

One of the most interesting things I learnt about working as a priest while at St Edmund's was something that had never been mentioned in the seminary. This was the fact that as a priest in a parish one never knew what might happen next. In a sense a priest has to be ready for anything. It could be the sudden death of a parishioner, a crisis arising within a family, an emergency at the local hospital, or a situation at the local school requiring the immediate ministrations of a priest. I was reminded of this recently when on our television screens, in our newspapers and on our radios we saw pictures and heard reports and interviews concerning forty schoolgirls (aged between thirteen and fifteen) caught on camera bullying one girl. As a consequence, all forty girls were suspended.

Until one of my duties at St Edmund's was to act as chaplain and part-time teacher at St Anne's, the large Catholic comprehensive school in the parish for 1,300 girls, I had never previously witnessed the phenomenon of large-scale bullying or indeed of real cruelty being inflicted by human beings on others. And then one day, during a break between lessons, I heard a terrible chanting noise coming from the school playground. I went to investigate.

On turning a corner I was horrified by what I saw. A black girl in her teens was standing with her back to a wall. She couldn't escape from where she stood because a semicircle of white girls had formed around her, cutting off her escape. It was these girls, about twenty of them, who were chanting in unison and urging on something that was going on in front of them.

What they were urging on were the actions of an Asian girl with an artificial arm which had a steel hook at the end of it in place of a hand, and who was standing next to the black girl. With this hook she was taunting and drawing closer all the time to the face of the black girl, frightening the life out of her.

I first let out a shocked bellow, which scattered the white girls and made them flee. I was unbelievably angry. With the semicircle broken, the black girl was then able to make her escape. She ran straight to me, shaking, sobbing and crying, and sprang into my arms, clinging to me. The Asian girl simply stood there saying nothing, with eyes looking down.

Cruelty is not the monopoly of any one section of human beings, no matter their age, race, colour or religion. And cruelty does not always take the form of physical bullying. It can be verbal. It may take the form of pouring scorn on someone, sneering at them, making so-called fun of them, mocking them or ganging up on them. It is so easy too to follow the crowd, to be part of a gang and to isolate an individual. On the other hand, it takes real courage to stand up for and befriend someone being mocked or bullied.

This was an important lesson I learnt at St Edmund's. Another was that so many people might believe in God but have little or no belief in their own self-worth. An even more common phenomenon, however, was and is the existence of so many people simply hostile to religion of any kind. After spending years in a seminary surrounded by believers, indeed devout practisers of their faith, this can come as an unpleasant shock to more than a few priests when they first encounter it.

I was surprised therefore when one day I received a visit from a young woman sent to me by her social worker. This woman was depressed and was seriously thinking of committing suicide. I had been advised not to mention either God or religion, since the woman was hostile to both. I did, however, persuade her to speak of how she viewed life and it was clear that she thought it odd to be talking to a priest.

Before she left she asked me what kind of things made me sad. In reply I took her to the window of my sitting room, which overlooked the busy streets of Southampton. I pointed to people rushing about doing their afternoon shopping, to others running to catch buses, to young men roaring past on motorcycles and so on. "How many of the people you see have given a thought to God today?" I asked her. "Perhaps a few, but not many," she replied. "That's what makes me sad," I said.

A few weeks later the young woman telephoned me to say she had begun to pray to God – the God I had been advised never to mention. She also told me that she had begun to spend her free time visiting people who were lonely, especially elderly people who were housebound.

But there were also occurrences that had their amusing side. I was to discover that these tend to balance the sad occurrences in the life of a priest and in fact lighten his days.

For example, it was the custom at Mass on Sundays at St Edmund's for the priest to read any banns of forthcoming marriages from the pulpit. On one memorable occasion, with a church full of parishioners, as I finished saying, "If anyone knows of any just cause or legal impediment why these two persons So-and-so and So-and-so should not be married, you should inform the priests as soon as possible", a middle-aged woman stood up and loudly proclaimed that she was utterly opposed to these two people whom I had named getting married. This had never happened to me before and no one had ever told me what to do if it did occur, but I told the woman to follow me into the sacristy or vestry and tell me her objections.

The woman began by declaring that the man in question would break the young woman's heart. I informed her that this was not a legal impediment. Not to be deterred, she went on to say that he had already broken several girls' hearts, and I repeated what I had just said. She then declared that the young man in question was a South American. To this I again replied that this was not a legal impediment, and suggested that we return to the body of the church and that she allow me to continue saying Mass.

When I returned from the sacristy the congregation was all agog, eager to know what the woman had said and what were her objections to the marriage. It took some time to remind them that we were in church and in the middle of Mass. Understandably the young couple who intended to marry and were in the congregation were also more than slightly upset.

It was at St Edmund's too that I first began to write, regarding this as a form of ministry or a way of spreading the Gospel. At first I was engaged to write a fortnightly column in *The Catholic Herald*, explaining to the general public the meaning and significance of the different documents that had emanated from the Second Vatican Council. Later I was also encouraged to write for *The Tablet*, the international Catholic weekly paper, by its editor, Tom Burns, who patiently taught me the rudiments of journalism. His successor, John Wilkins, would later enlist me in the late 1980s as the anonymous writer of the "Pastor Ignotus" column for three years.

On one occasion when I was writing my column for *The Catholic Herald*, for some mysterious reason the pen in my hand would not stop writing. Each time I tried to stop, ideas simply seemed determined to flow. This had never happened to me before and I found the experience both strange and inexplicable. It was also embarrassing because I was about to visit Quarr Abbey on the Isle of Wight to make my annual spiritual retreat, so I hastily put a wodge of paper in my bag and set off to catch the ferry.

For the next week, whenever I was not actually in the monastery church praying or in the refectory eating, I sat in my cell feeling compelled to write. Little did I realise that I was actually writing my very first book, which was later – with an introduction by Michael Hollings – to be published under the title of *Listening with the Heart.*

This occurred in 1976, the year after Henry Clarke, the priest who had not only received me into the Catholic Church but who was also my regular confessor, had tragically died of leukaemia, so I was anxiously searching for a priest to take on this role. I thought it important to find a priest with whom I could be completely open and honest, talk about anything under the sun, confess my sins with total confidence, and from whom I could receive wise advice. Without such a person, commonly known as a spiritual director, the life of a celibate priest could sometimes be lonely.

In my case, my search for a priest, such as Henry had been, was largely motivated by my wish to ensure that I was, in a sense, fully alive. In other words – as I had confided to Bishop Worlock the night before my ordination – I needed to know that as a celibate priest my emotions were not atrophying, but being fully utilised in my understanding of those whom I was called to serve.

During all my five years in the seminary in Rome and at the Gregorian University there, I could not recall any occasion, except a light-hearted one in a student debate, when celibacy had even been mentioned. It was as though it was a taboo subject, and we were all expected to live a celibate life without preparation or guidance.

Celibacy is generally talked of by many lay people as something that enables a priest to be of service to all without family priorities interfering in his total dedication and commitment to Christ and his work. This notion is true.

At other times celibacy is spoken of as a discipline that allows a bishop to move priests around his diocese without having to take into account a priest's family responsibilities. This has sometimes resulted in priests being moved on the grounds of obedience to the bishop without consideration for, let alone consultation as to, their wishes.

Sometimes but not often the matter of money might come into the discussion of celibacy, and it is a fact that the cost to the Church of employing married clergy, possibly with children requiring education, would be considerably higher than at present. (Convert Anglican married clergy, functioning as Catholic priests, are usually employed in positions to which there is a salary automatically attached, such as prison or hospital chaplaincy.)

The theological basis for priestly celibacy is different. It is based in the study of what are called the Last Things, that is, death and our final destiny. Here celibacy is considered as a sign of contradiction, in other words a sign to others that this world is not all there is to life but simply a preface as it were, albeit an extremely important one, to a life hereafter in which, as Jesus said, there is no giving and taking in marriage. It is actually a noble idea and is supposed to remind people of higher things. Often, however, this idea is not explained and leaves many lay men and women no wiser. Some priests indeed find celibacy a form of martyrdom.

Personally I was and am able to accept all of these reasons for celibacy, especially as I could not imagine anyone in my own life occupying in both my heart and mind as prominent a place as Jesus Christ. On the other hand, I was and am adamant that a celibate priest should of necessity have close friends, who understand as far as possible the priestly life and to whom he can turn for support at all times. And throughout my priestly life I have been blessed with such friends.

I had seen too many good priests whose celibacy had taken the form of a suppressant of their emotions, instead of enabling them to empathise with the problems and dilemmas, as well as joys, of their parishioners. I knew therefore that Henry Clarke would be a tall order to follow as a confessor and spiritual director, and so far the search for a suitable substitute had been in vain.

At Quarr Abbey, where I had gone for a retreat, Mass each morning was celebrated in Latin by all the monks together in the monastery's astonishingly beautiful church. Although invited to join them, I, however, said Mass by myself in the church's crypt. Apparently one day the monk who for that week was the main celebrant of the community's Mass enquired of the guest master why I said Mass alone. I gently told the guest master that I found it easier to pray in English and was subsequently told that the chief celebrant had then enquired if I would join the monks the following day if they had Mass in English. Surprised by this offer, I obviously said yes.

After celebrating Mass with the community the following day, I made enquiries about Leo Avery, the monk who had made this kind gesture, and, after reflection and observation, decided to ask him to become my regular confessor, so asked the guest master if I could speak with Leo. The next day he knocked on the door of my cell.

From the very first I was struck by Leo's humility. He had no idea why I had asked to see him (apparently no guest had done so for the past three years), and he presumed that I had some question to ask him to do with the scriptures, as he had not long since returned from completing biblical studies in Rome. When I asked instead if he would become my regular confessor, he literally began to shake. He clearly considered the request more significant than I imagined and asked if he could have time to reflect on the matter. It was then my turn to be astonished by a succession of events.

In a parish one rarely had time to think, let alone reflect, before being asked to hear a person's confession and I knew of no priest who ever refused, but I agreed to Leo's plea for time. I did tell him, however, that

I was leaving the following day, so that gave him only twenty-four hours to come to a decision.

A few hours later I was amazed to be visited in turn in my cell by both the abbot and the prior, his deputy. Clearly Leo had told them of my request. To my astonishment they both thought my request a splendid idea and asked me to persevere with my request. When I asked why, they replied that it would be an excellent way for Leo to obtain pastoral experience, since they both hoped that one day he would become abbot. I couldn't help thinking that my needs were not exactly what they had in mind!

Shortly before my departure from the monastery the next day, Leo appeared at my door. He said that he would become my regular confessor, suggesting that I visit the monastery for this purpose once a month, but this was only on one condition. Somewhat taken aback, I enquired as to the nature of the condition. He said the condition was that I should become his regular confessor! And so for the next eighteen years, as Leo subsequently took on one role after another at Quarr – procurator or bursar, guest master, prior and finally abbot – we met once a month to discuss matters of mutual interest and to shrive each other. In so doing it was inevitable that we became close friends. Ultimately I preached at his installation as abbot and not many years later rushed to the hospital on the Isle of Wight when he was diagnosed as suffering from a tumour on the brain. He died on the operating table and I have never since been back to Quarr.

After five years at St Edmund's I was subsequently sent in 1977 as curate or assistant priest to Chandler's Ford, which was an urban development between Southampton and Winchester in Hampshire. In those days, there was no such thing as discussion or consultation between a junior priest and his bishop beforehand, one simply received a letter from the bishop instructing one to move within days to a different parish. In the event this proved an unhappy time for me.

The parish priest at Chandler's Ford had never had an assistant before, let alone someone of forty-three, and was determined not only to exert his authority but to oversee in detail my every pastoral activity, which I had no choice but to carry out in the evenings after continuing to teach during the day at the girls' school in Southampton. Inevitably there was often unspoken friction between us and it was clear that he did not want me living in the parish presbytery. Instead I was placed in a maisonette on a housing estate some distance from the church.

Shortly before moving to Chandler's Ford I had also moved my mother, now in her late eighties, from near Dover in Kent to a flat in Southampton, and felt not only duty-bound but increasingly responsible for her welfare. It was now that she started attending Mass on Sundays at least and becoming unhappy at not being able to receive Holy Communion as she had always done as an Anglican. Fortunately I was aided in the care of my mother by the Sisters of the Order of Our Lady of Charity, who regularly visited her and gave her hospitality most weekends. These were the same nuns I had first got to know in their work among children in care.

Things in the parish came to a head between the parish priest and myself the very first Christmas I was there, when he announced that he alone would decide precisely what percentage of the Christmas collection I should receive. By a long-standing custom throughout the diocese, collections at Christmas and Easter in every parish were divided equally between all the clergy resident in the parish, so I made no bones about telling him what I thought about his decision. After that I began to consider how I could obtain a move to another parish.

It was not long afterwards that I was approached by the rector of Allen Hall, the major seminary in London for the training of priests, and asked if I would be prepared to move there and lecture in church history. Given my situation, I expressed interest and was duly summoned to a meeting with Bishop Anthony Emery, the Bishop of Portsmouth at the time, who had received a letter from Cardinal Hume supporting the rector in his request.

When the bishop enquired whether I really wanted to go to Allen Hall, I replied that it all depended on how long he intended to keep me at Chandler's Ford. Without my having to explain why I had put the matter thus, Bishop Emery understood the situation immediately. He then asked how I would respond if he were to make me a parish priest the following September and combine that office with becoming the diocesan inspector of religious education in all its secondary schools in Hampshire, Berkshire, the Channel Islands and the Isle of Wight. When I showed my enthusiasm for this, he gently remarked that in the eyes of the parish priest of Chandler's Ford this would look like promotion for his curate and therefore he could bathe in a certain amount of reflected glory. This proved to be the case and faces were saved all round.

For the next thirteen years I spent a great deal of time travelling the length and breadth of the Portsmouth diocese inspecting and reporting on religious education in Catholic secondary schools, both voluntary-aided and independent. For good measure I was also required to sit on the Hampshire County Council Committee for Education as the representative of the Roman Catholic Church and listen to endless rather tedious debates among politicians.

Needless to say in September 1978 I was immensely happy to arrive as parish priest at Bishop's Waltham, a rural parish, relatively close to Portsmouth and consisting of sixteen villages. The actual church was close to the ruins of the medieval palace where William of Wykeham, the founder of Winchester College and New College, Oxford, had died. My five years there were to prove wonderfully fulfilling.

The parish may have been relatively poor compared to the two previous parishes in which I had served, but it was hugely rich in its cross section of parishioners from all kinds of different backgrounds, ranging from naval personnel and retired professional people to salt-of-the-earth working-class men and women. As previously at both Chandler's Ford and Southampton, there were specific individuals or families in the parish who provided one with friendship and moral support when the going was hard, and who also shamed one by the depth of their Christian faith and practice. At Bishop's Waltham this was particularly so of a retired and devoted married couple, called Eunice and Fred Cook.

Whereas Eunice acted as a dedicated sacristan, Fred was assiduous in his care of the church building and its grounds. What, however, made them memorable was the extent to which they made sure that everyone in the parish, including me, and often those outside it, wanted for nothing in times of both sickness and health, whether it was the basic things of life or human friendship. It was this element of caring that ran like a thread through all the parish celebrations of the different sacraments whether it was daily Mass, weddings, baptisms, the reception of newcomers into the Church or the celebration of the sacrament of reconciliation.

It was at Bishop's Waltham too that I had my mother, now ninety years of age, to live with me after her doctor had diagnosed her as having myeloma and being unable any longer to live on her own. Almost as strong willed as ever and retaining many of her north-country characteristics, my mother was not content to sit back and rest despite requiring round-the-clock care. She constantly wanted to know what was going on in the parish and expressed her opinions without reserve. Eventually, however, the local doctor advised me that, unless I ceased trying to nurse my mother at night and carry out my parish and educational duties by day, I could easily be the first to die! I conceded that he might be right and agreed to his arranging for my mother to live with and be cared for by the Sisters of Nazareth in Southampton, where I and my friends were able to visit her daily.

It was at Nazareth House that my mother began attending daily Mass and on one celebrated occasion asked me why the priest there never gave her Holy Communion but passed her by. When I tried gently to explain that he was unable to give her communion because he was aware that she was not a Catholic, she retorted that "Jesus would not pass me by!" to which I could provide no adequate response.

Shortly after this episode my mother broke the news to me that she would like to become a Catholic. Stupidly I asked whether this was because I was a Catholic priest, after which there was an ominous silence to be broken by my mother trenchantly informing me that she was talking about herself, not me. The problem was that someone seeking to become a Catholic is usually required to undertake a fairly lengthy course of instruction in the faith, whereas in my mother's case one didn't know, largely because of the myeloma (mercifully painless), how much longer she would live. Under the circumstances I approached Bishop Emery and, after I explained the situation, his only concern was whether my mother believed in the Real Presence. When I replied that this was precisely what the matter was all about, he told me unhesitatingly to receive my mother into the Catholic Church. This response was one for which I would remain hugely indebted to him.

It is a remarkable experience to receive one's mother into the Church. Whereas I was almost nervous about it, I was amazed by the way she entered deeply and calmly into the event without fuss or astonishment. Clearly for her it was simply a progression on a path she had been bent on pursuing all her life – a more profound understanding and experience of the Real Presence of Christ in Holy Communion. She was to die peacefully the following year, surrounded by nuns and myself, having received the sacrament of anointing, formerly known as the last rites, from the Nazareth House chaplain.

One of the major problems at Bishop's Waltham, as in all rural Catholic parishes, was that the most natural community for most parishioners was the village in which they lived and were often ultimately buried, whereas for worship they were required to attend the Catholic church at Bishop's Waltham. It was not always easy, therefore, to create a sense of community when people usually only met one another once a week for Mass. Then, after five years in what I termed this idyllic parish, I naively approached Bishop Emery in 1983 and asked him to give me a challenge, a request to which he immediately agreed. Thereafter I vowed never again to ask a bishop for a challenge!

The challenging task that the bishop gave me was to move to the city of Portsmouth, to combine two neighbouring parishes – St Colman's at Cosham and St Paul's at Paulsgrove – into one, and to be the parish priest of both. This meant that I had charge of two churches, two presbyteries and two church halls. Within the combined parishes there was also a large hospital and a Catholic primary school. I was assisted in all this by an elderly curate who acted as the hospital chaplain. In theory this was fine; in fact, however, one parish was affluent and middle class, and the other poor and chiefly working class, living on housing estates built after the Second World War to house families that had been bombed out of their homes. The bishop was now asking me to unite two quite different types of parish in which none of the people involved looked favourably on the proposed union. To put it bluntly, the affluent middle-class section resented sharing their money and resources with the poor part, whilst the working-class area did not wish to be beholden to the affluent. It did not take me long to become convinced that wherever parishes are amalgamated sociological differences need to be taken into account.

In order to deal with the situation as quickly as possible, I managed, however, to persuade the provincial or head of the Sisters of Our Lady of Charity in England – the order I had come to know well from my days in Southampton – to send a group of her nuns to live in the presbytery at Paulsgrove and work as paid parish assistants there. At Cosham I gradually recruited volunteer lay men and women to be pastorally responsible for different parts of the parish in the areas where they lived. This was delegation and shared responsibility on a huge scale, but it worked. For the administration and celebration of the sacraments my assistant and I moved between both areas.

The nuns at Paulsgrove proved to be a godsend and they were utterly appreciated and loved by the parishioners there. Not only did they lead the worship at church, take Holy Communion to elderly housebound and sick people, and form support groups including a prayer group, but they liaised with the headmistress of the local Catholic school in order to lend assistance to parents or families in need. They also visited people in their homes, advising and assisting them in all sorts of practical ways. On one memorable occasion I recall visiting a parishioner during the night on being informed that her husband had just died, only to find that the nuns were already there laying out the man's body. Nothing was either too much or too menial for them to undertake on behalf of the people of Paulsgrove, and it was nothing short of a tragedy when a successor of mine terminated their stay in the parish.

Sadly I have to admit that, during the seven years from 1983 to 1990 that I lived and worked in Portsmouth, friction between the Cosham and Paulsgrove parts of the parish never completely disappeared. Although in their different ways many parishioners from both parts were stalwarts of the Catholic faith, on the social level they were as different as chalk and cheese, and either could not or would not join together in harmony. At times this could be heartbreaking, not least because it seemed contrary to the Gospel.

It was also during these years, however, that I developed a love of America. This partly occurred because during this time I found myself at one stage being invited, as the vice chairman of the National Conference of Priests of England and Wales, to address the annual convention of all the priests of North America gathered in San Antonio in Texas.

Unfortunately from the start of this visit I took an instant dislike to the priests in Texas, acting as hosts at the convention. The accommodation and arrangements for the convention could not have been better organised. Our hosts could not have been more welcoming and hospitable. What I irrationally did not appreciate was their wearing of large Stetson hats and cowboy boots, riding in huge limousines, and in loud voices boasting about the wonders of Texas. I could not get over how they kept telling me that I must be enjoying myself because I was in Texas and how proud they were that the battle of the Alamo had been fought at San Antonio. They were particularly taken aback that I had not seen the film about the Alamo starring John Wayne. By the end of the week, when I was supposed to give an address to the four hundred delegates from every Catholic diocese in America, both they and I were heartily tired of our hosts. In order to satisfy the Texans, however, I decided early on that I should visit the site of the Alamo, look round the museum about it, see the film and examine Davy Crockett's hat, a relic of the battle.

When it came to the time for me to address the convention at which the Texan hosts were sitting in the front row, I could not resist beginning my speech by informing the gathering that I had indeed visited the battle site. The Texans smiled with pride and the other delegates stifled a yawn. Then I said that I had noticed on a war memorial that thirteen Englishmen had died in the battle and I wondered why they had been so far from home. Finally I added that I had read the inscription on the memorial to the effect that "they had died for liberty and Texas". Out loud I remarked that, whereas I could understand why anyone would die for liberty, it defeated me why they would be prepared to die for Texas! It was at this point that all hell was let loose. The Texans in the front row were red in the face and furious. They looked as though they might storm the platform and set about me, whilst the four hundred delegates were initially stunned into silence, making me think for a moment that I had committed the biggest mistake of my life. Then, like a huge wave crashing onto a shoreline, the priests behind the Texans began clapping and cheering, standing on their chairs and waving, applauding and jumping up and down. After that they were prepared to accept anything I said as Gospel truth, even that the moon was made of cheese. It was an experience I would never forget.

Another incident, which brought all of us attending the convention very quickly down to earth, occurred during a Mass being celebrated in the local cathedral by the Bishop of San Antonio. During his homily, which was very simple and straightforward, it became apparent that the majority of these four hundred priests, who represented the cream of the American Catholic Church, were bored with what the bishop was saying and would have preferred it if he had engaged in some intellectual fireworks. Then the bishop, sensing the atmosphere, suddenly stopped and pointed across the sanctuary to where another bishop was seated. Pointing to this other bishop, he said that there was a friend of his from Nicaragua, who spoke no English. In recent times, he went on, this bishop had seen more than a few of his priests shot or arrested, members of religious orders working in his diocese had disappeared, and many lay catechists had been imprisoned or tortured. He had come to San Antonio and this convention in particular to find replacements for his priests who had been killed. Then, on behalf of his fellow bishop, the Bishop of San Antonio asked for volunteers from the congregation to stand up and be prepared to return to Nicaragua with his friend.

We all, without exception, felt very small. Five priests out of the four hundred stood up and volunteered.

Again in my capacity as vice chairman of the National Conference of Priests of England and Wales I was on one occasion invited to give a lecture at St Benet's in Oxford, the private hall of residence originally established for Benedictine monks from Ampleforth. It was during dinner after the lecture that a young tall American monk from a Benedictine monastery in California leant across the table and surprised me by asking if I would become his regular confessor. This was Luke Dysinger, a qualified medical doctor and, as I was to discover, an amazingly intelligent and knowledgeable postgraduate, studying theology at Oxford in preparation for his ordination to the priesthood in three years' time.

I explained that I lived in Portsmouth, seventy miles from Oxford, so it would not be easy for us to meet. Then, obviously not seeing this as a difficulty, he came up with the idea of visiting Portsmouth once a month, staying the night in my presbytery, going to confession and Mass the following day, and then returning to Oxford. This he did for the next three years. It also meant that through him I came to know and visit his monastery, St Andrew's at Valyermo in the Mohave Desert in southern California, which I later wrote about in a book entitled *Fully Alive*.

After visiting California in the mid 1980s and being made aware of the nascent AIDS epidemic, I had also taken to doing research and lecturing on the subject to priests, doctors and nurses, teachers and the general public throughout England. This was done with the active encouragement of Cardinal Hume, whom I represented at a conference of people working in the field of AIDS at the Vatican. There I first made the acquaintance of Cardinal O'Connor of New York, who would appear later in my story.

One of the saddest events concerning AIDS to come my way during these years was when I received a phone call one day from an organisation in London offering support to the relatives of men and women suffering from AIDS. I was asked over the phone if I knew anyone who could go to a widow, who was living alone and was an invalid in a wheelchair in a south-coast resort, and break the news to her that her only son, who was a doctor, was dying of AIDS. I said I would ring them back if I could think of anyone.

I thought about this long and hard and then phoned a university lecturer I knew, called John (not his real name), living in the same town as the widow. When he heard the situation he volunteered to break the news to the woman himself, and he did.

A week later I was shocked to receive a letter from John telling me that he himself had AIDS and was in St Mary's Hospital, Paddington. I immediately put the holy oils for anointing the sick in my briefcase, as well as the Blessed Sacrament, and caught the first train to London. When I reached the hospital I was a bit worried, because I knew from experience that the facial appearance of people with AIDS changes as the disease progresses. I was concerned that I would not recognise John. I need not have worried, however; he saw me first when I entered a ward full of people with AIDS.

I sat down by his bedside and asked how I could best help him. He said he wanted to make his confession, then receive the sacrament of the sick (that is, be anointed with oil on the hands and forehead), and then receive Holy Communion. From then on I made the journey to London once a week and watched as the disease steadily took hold of him.

First he lost a huge amount of weight, then the virus attacked his brain and he began to hallucinate and go blind. But in that London hospital I witnessed such care and compassion for those who were sick and dying as I'd never seen before. Finally John died, and in his will asked that I should officiate at his funeral.

Since 1981, when the HIV virus was first discovered, more than 25 million people in our world have died of AIDS. In 2007, 33 million people worldwide were HIV-positive and over 12 million children have been made orphans as a result of AIDS. Around the world more than 6,000 young people fall ill with HIV every day.

I had always maintained that anyone working in the front line of the field of AIDS should work no more than three years at a time, owing to the danger of them experiencing what is known as burnout. It was never easy watching men and women, especially the young, dying from this incurable disease. So in 1990, when I was invited to spend a sabbatical year at Georgetown University in Washington DC teaching and doing research in history, I accepted the invitation.

Even though I said my farewells to parishioners and friends, I little realised that I would never get to Georgetown and that I would never again be a parish priest.

6

Oxford chaplain

Early one morning in the summer of 1990, as I was reflecting that it was time I bought my air ticket to Washington DC, I received a telephone call from the Bishop of Portsmouth, Crispian Hollis, who had succeeded Anthony Emery. He asked me to come and see him that day. When I arrived, he immediately informed me that the Catholic chaplain to Oxford University had resigned, after being in office for only one year. He asked if I would be prepared to forgo my sabbatical in America and, instead, become the chaplain at Oxford, reminding me that I knew the ropes, having studied there twice, first as an undergraduate and then as a postgraduate.

My first thought was to wonder whether I would be able to fill an office I remembered so vividly being filled by Michael Hollings, my first spiritual director and the person who had influenced me most to become a priest. I asked the bishop if I could sleep on his request. I first wanted to consult Leo Avery, now the Abbot of Quarr. Having done so, the following day I rang the bishop and agreed to go to Oxford rather than America.

Looking back I can appreciate that if I had not gone to Oxford my life – after a sabbatical in America – would probably have continued to be that of a parish priest. This would not have disappointed me because I had come to appreciate, during the previous eighteen years in parish work, that being of service to others was uniquely rewarding. When people in one's parish were facing tragedies, suffering from incurable diseases or undergoing bereavement, one plumbed the depths of compassion on their behalf. When they were experiencing immense happiness on the occasion of their marriage or the birth of their children, one participated in their joy. At such times I came to realise how privileged I was to be a priest. Moreover, my brother priests were often unique and dedicated characters, who were usually there to support one when needed and always able to bring one down to earth when one felt proud or had become obnoxious. This did not mean that there were not times when I was frustrated, sometimes lonely, angry or disappointed, but never once did I regret becoming a priest.

On going to Oxford, however, I was to discover that to be an undergraduate and postgraduate at Oxford was one thing, but to be the Catholic chaplain to the university was a totally different matter. Whereas I thoroughly enjoyed and never once regretted being available to serve the myriad needs of the students, whether it involved, as it frequently did, their relationships with one another, or problems to do with their families, their studies, their accommodation, finance and indeed anything whatsoever, I found that – with honourable exceptions – dealing with their teachers, known as dons or senior members of the university, was not so pleasant.

The academic world on the inside was not as I hoped or imagined. Moreover, in the intervening twenty-odd years since I had studied there as a postgraduate, Oxford itself had changed. Certainly Christianity at Oxford was now very much on the decline. In 1954, when I first went up as an undergraduate, religion at my college was taken very seriously and indeed attendance in chapel on a Sunday had been compulsory. Now, in the early 1990s, there was discussion in more than a few colleges about how college chapels could be put to alternative use, such as becoming libraries, common rooms, or even accommodation for students. Some dons were asking whether their college should continue to employ a college chaplain at all and even more dons were behind the advance of secularism throughout the university.

What might be called a forgetfulness of God, and an almost exclusive concern for worldly success, were beginning to bite. Memories of former days when Oxford had been a beacon of Christianity were little more than parts of a rapidly fading dream. Dons such as my former postgraduate supervisor, John Walsh of Jesus College, who was a veritable pillar of Christian living and a mentor to so many, were becoming scarce on the ground.

More than a few of the dons were instead obsessed with their own little worlds and academic subjects, jealous of each other's achievements, petty-minded and ungenerous. I should have known this from my past reading of the novels of C.P. Snow or from listening to my friend Tony Battle, who had turned down the opportunity of becoming the chaplain at Cambridge, choosing Newcastle University instead. Under the circumstances, I was frequently reminded at this time of the apocryphal story of the appointment of a young man to a fellowship of a particular Oxford college.

Following the young man's appointment, the head of the college offered to give him a conducted tour of the college and, as they were going around, the young man felt obliged to show off his learning and abilities. After a while, and stopping him in his tracks, the head of the college said, "You don't have to show you're clever, you know. We're all clever here. Try to be kind, that's much more difficult and much more rare here."

For me it became a constant battle to persuade some of the dons to lift their eyes above the politics of the privileged, gated and walled quadrangles of the thirty or so mostly ancient colleges comprising the university. I especially disliked the attitude of those who referred to the undergraduates as "children", wishing they would soon go home and leave them to write their books and to continue with their researches. I found their inward-looking attitude frequently uncongenial and smug, but of course there were still many dons who were exceedingly kind and concerned for the welfare of their students, such as the Warden of Keble College, Professor Averil Cameron, among others.

In order to celebrate my appointment to Oxford, a former parishioner of mine from Bishop's Waltham parish, a former naval captain and now First Sea Lord, Admiral Sir Julian Oswald, and his wife, Roni, kindly laid on a small dinner party for me at his official residence in the arch at the end of the Mall in London, which stretches from Buckingham Palace to Trafalgar Square. He and Roni had become valued friends over the years, together with their five children whom I had watched grow up, marry and have children of their own. Julian refused to say who the other guests were to be, but I was given instructions to arrive early in order to greet them as they arrived.

On the evening in question I stood by the entrance and was taken aback when the first guests to arrive were Cardinal Hume and his secretary; the next was the Apostolic Nuncio, Archbishop Barbarito; then a future peer, Sir Charles Powell, and his Italian wife, Carla; and finally the senior naval chaplain, Jed Lavender, who hailed from Newcastle. Together with Julian and Roni Oswald we comprised a small and intimate gathering and I was delighted to find myself seated next to the charming, elegant and ebullient Carla Powell.

Obviously Carla Powell and I spent much of the evening reminiscing about Rome and all things Italian, so much so that at one point I forgot where I was and innocently asked for her telephone number. This seemed to please her and she immediately reached under the table for her handbag in order to fish for an address card. It was then that everyone at the table fell silent and to my utter embarrassment stared at me. I had no idea what to say by way of explanation and felt my cheeks burning with all eyes upon me. It was then that the First Sea Lord completely rescued me by observing that he had always wanted that phone number but that it took a priest to have the courage to ask for it. Everyone laughed, Carla came from under the table wondering but probably guessing what all the fuss was about, and I kept my eyes on the plate before me.

In subsequent weeks, months and years Charles and Carla Powell became two of my closest friends, visiting Oxford from time to time, besides frequently providing both food and clothes for students in need, especially those from overseas. That supper in London remained one of the happiest occasions during my time as chaplain, just as later I enjoyed officiating at the wedding of Charles and Carla Powell's youngest son in France and being flown there for the first and only time in a private jet, alongside such celebrities as Peter Mandelson, the government minister; Lord Birt, the Director-General of the BBC at the time; Carol Thatcher and other *glitterati*.

The chaplaincy, like that at Cambridge, had been specifically founded in the late nineteenth century to ensure that Catholic members of the university received not only pastoral assistance during the period of their studies, but orthodox Catholic teaching. The chaplain was appointed precisely to bring this latter into his Sunday sermons.

The chaplaincy itself was and still is housed in an old Elizabethan house called the Old Palace in St Aldate's Street, opposite Christ Church meadows and close to the city centre. It was reputed to have been the residence of the first Anglican Bishop of Oxford in the sixteenth century. It may have been a listed building and picturesque, with walls made of wattle instead of bricks and a long but undistinguished history, but it was draughty, noisy and inconvenient. Attached to it Michael Hollings had built accommodation for a dozen or so students.

During my tenure at the chaplaincy, and at different times, I had one or two distinguished priest colleagues to assist me, as well as at one time a delightful woman who belonged to the Teresian lay association and, at another, a high-flying academic nun who had previously served as a university chaplain. These, together with a quiet and efficient administrator, a cook and a cleaner, all strove to put themselves at the service of the Catholic students of the university.

Once a year I was required to appear before members of what was known as the Newman Trust, the body legally responsible for the running of the chaplaincy, and give a report of what had occurred at the chaplaincy during the previous academic year. This body comprised senior Catholic members of the university. They determined how much finance was available for the day-to-day expenses of the chaplaincy, as well as the salaries of its staff, including me. Either because they regarded it as a privilege to be appointed a chaplain at Oxford or because they were under the misapprehension that a chaplain had a private income, the trustees expected a chaplain to survive on a very low salary, even lower than when one was working in a parish. This made it necessary during vacations to supplement one's salary with other work, such as giving retreats or writing. This is what both Monsignor Ronald Knox and Michael Hollings had done before me.

Nevertheless, my time as chaplain to the university was on the whole thoroughly enjoyable and fulfilling. Besides feeling as though one was contributing and assisting to the development in early adulthood of so many future Catholic citizens, one found life in such a city as Oxford full of cultural opportunities of all kinds to widen one's own horizons. Even though one often faced difficulties of the kind already mentioned, they rarely detracted from the joy of seeing and enabling students to grow especially in their spiritual lives, particularly through prayer and frequenting the sacraments. I was often amazed by the extent of students' concern for underprivileged and deprived people, their attitude often putting older generations to shame. This was so much so that many of the students that I first encountered at Oxford subsequently became some of my most valued friends and in later years I derived immense pleasure from officiating at their weddings or at the baptism of their children, sometimes as far afield as America, Canada, France and Germany.

On one occasion I particularly recall that an American postgraduate medical student at Oxford announced that, if ever he got married, he wanted me to be present when he proposed to the girl in question. I and those listening thought this a strange and not serious statement and quickly forgot it, until a few years later I received a telephone call from Greece from this same young man.

Now a qualified doctor and shortly to become a consultant, he informed me that he was on holiday with his girlfriend, but that they would be passing through England on their way home and would like to meet me for lunch. We went to a restaurant and the moment we were seated he began to propose to her. Taken aback, I stopped him and demanded to know what he was doing. He then said that he was simply fulfilling what he called the vow he had made at Oxford that I should be present when he offered his hand in marriage to the girl of his choice.

In response to this, I then ordered him to do the job properly and to get down on his knees. He did so, much to the amusement of those in the restaurant, customers and staff alike, not least because I was presiding over this ceremony dressed in my dog collar and black suit.

The girl responded "Yes" to his earnest request, and promptly burst into tears. The young man then reached into his pocket and produced the largest diamond ring I had ever seen. Placing it on her finger, she declared she would wear it for ever, everyone in the restaurant applauded and, red-faced, I ordered the young man to get off his knees. The couple then promptly embraced.

Emerging from each other's arms they then invited me to officiate at their wedding in San Diego in California the following summer and to fly there at their expense. This I was happy to do, but other students were to do equally memorable things and astonish me.

It was my custom of a weekday evening to visit all the different Oxford colleges in turn and say Mass for the Catholics who lived there, but on one occasion for some inexplicable reason I was reluctant to do so, and in fact for the first time ever did not feel like saying Mass. As I made my way to Trinity College, my destination that particular evening, my mood became increasingly truculent. The result was that when I arrived at the college chapel I was – uncharacteristically – not happy to see a group of students who were gathered around the organ.

Assuming them all to be Catholics gathered for the Mass, I immediately began giving them particular tasks to do. I told one that she would be reading from the scriptures that evening, another that he would be leading the bidding prayers, the third that she should prepare to bring the bread and wine to the altar at the appropriate time in the Mass, and finally I informed another, who told me in an unmistakably Irish accent that his name was Andrew, that he would be preaching a sermon for us. Now this latter was not only unheard of and forbidden in the Catholic Church, but it was an indication that I was totally out of sorts. Because of my mood none of the students felt able to protest about my instructions, apart from the fact that there were surreptitious grins all round, which I stupidly interpreted as the emanations of overgrown adolescents!

All went well until we reached the sermon. I then told the assembled gathering of students to sit down and I gestured to Andrew to stand and preach. Without any hesitation Andrew stood up and launched into one of the most serious, compelling and heartfelt sermons I had ever heard. The thing that disturbed me most, however, was the fact that he kept frequently plucking biblical texts out of his memory to support his argument, and clearly he had done this sort of thing before. I knew that few Catholic students would know their Bible as well as Andrew and it was obvious that he was a gifted and experienced preacher. It was then that I realised that Andrew was in fact a convinced Protestant from Northern Ireland.

Appreciating the irony of the whole situation, my mood immediately altered to one of sheer joy. Before the end of the Mass I publicly apologised to everyone for my previous bad mood and told Andrew that to make amends I ought to take him out to dinner sometime in the future. In front of all his friends (originally gathered not for Mass but at the conclusion of a college choir practice), he then retorted, "How about tomorrow night?" To this I sheepishly replied, "Yes". And so began the most amazing and wonderful Christian friendship. For the rest of his time at Oxford Andrew was a regular and popular visitor at the chaplaincy. He introduced me to his parents and brothers when they visited from Northern Ireland and a few years later I attended his wedding. Today I continue to be in touch with him, his wife and two small sons.

Evidence of students' interest in the plight of dispossessed people surfaced strongly during several occasions while I was chaplain. The first was their participation in an inter-denominational week-long university mission, which I had helped to organise with a group of Anglican chaplains, and which had as its main contributors Archbishop Desmond Tutu and Jean Vanier. Every evening of the mission they addressed packed gatherings of students. Another important event was a visit from Cardinal John O'Connor, the Archbishop of New York, whom I had first met at the conference on AIDS at the Vatican and who gave a stimulating and inspiring lecture on the state of the Catholic

Church at that time. He was, however, critical of the fact that in his view Oxford was utterly and irretrievably liberal. Mother Teresa also visited Oxford while I was chaplain and, to a huge audience at the Oxford Union, spoke of the evils of abortion, brooking no contradiction.

One of the most positive events for me at this time was the formation of the Catholic Students' Society or CathSoc, alongside the older and more traditional Newman Society. The Catholic Society was energetically organised by a student called Dominic Howarth, who later became a priest for the diocese of Brentwood and served with distinction as the diocesan youth officer. The work of CathSoc ensured that most of the academic and social activities of Catholic students were catered for. This is not to mention the other spiritual, biblical, musical and liturgical groups that thrived and held their meetings at the chaplaincy each week in term time.

It was estimated that in the early 1990s there were approximately a thousand Catholic undergraduates at Oxford, of whom about seven hundred frequented the chaplaincy in term time. The remainder either no longer practised their faith or chose to attend Mass at such religious private halls of residence or places of worship as those belonging to the Dominicans, the Oratory Fathers, the Benedictines, Opus Dei, the Franciscans and the Jesuits. Indeed Oxford was and is blessed with the presence of many religious orders. Among all of them I was invariably made welcome and accepted as a colleague and friend. There were occasions, however, when I was decidedly challenged as chaplain.

I distinctly remember preaching one Sunday evening at the chaplaincy when I was interrupted halfway through my sermon by a woman known throughout the city. Sadly this woman was a beggar and an alcoholic and on this occasion she was drunk. She stood up, approached the lectern where I was preaching, shouted abuse, began singing, heckled whenever I opened my mouth and laughed in a demonic fashion. I asked her to sit down, offered to listen to her and discuss whatever she liked after the service, but she adamantly refused. Then she did sit down but continued interrupting.

Meanwhile I began to get impatient, even angry inside, but realised the importance of keeping calm. This was especially so because the congregation at this particular Mass of about two hundred students was watching me intently to see how I would handle the situation. Then I deliberately changed tactics and asked how her son was. The woman promptly burst into tears. Her son apparently was in hospital suffering from pneumonia, having slept outdoors in bitterly cold weather. He also was what we euphemistically call "a man of the road".

At that point two nuns got up and attempted to escort the woman out of the church, an action the woman did not appreciate and which made her even more abusive. It also made the students uneasy. I stopped the nuns from proceeding whereupon the woman moved among the choir and, coming across a student called Danny, commenced singing "Oh Danny Boy" at the top of her voice. Finally, declaring that we were all hypocrites, she left.

The following day I encountered the same woman in the street. She came up to me with a huge grin on her face and said, "Ah, sure Father, we had a grand time yesterday, didn't we?"

I replied, "No, but I know what you mean."

Despite many happy events occurring during my six years as chaplain at Oxford, I was looking forward to the end of my contract and to being able to return to parish life, but providence had other things in store for me.

7

Eton

One day in late 1995, as I sat at my desk beneath the large portrait in oils of Monsignor Ronald Knox in the drawing room of the chaplaincy at Oxford, the telephone rang and I picked it up.

"Hello," I said.

"Good morning," came the reply. "This is Camoys, *Lord* Camoys."

"Yes, I know," I said, determined not to sound impressed.

"I was wondering if you ever come to town?" he replied. (To describe London in this way, as though those of us who lived elsewhere were country bumpkins, was guaranteed to upset me, but to be fair he was not to know this.)

Through semi-gritted teeth and rather loftily, I said, "I come to London when I have something *specific* to do and then return to Oxford immediately."

"Would lunch at Boodle's next Wednesday be sufficiently specific?" he asked. (Clever, I thought, quite apart from the fact that I had never seen the inside of Boodle's, a famous gentlemen's club founded in the eighteenth century in St James's Street.)

"Yes, that sounds very specific to me," I responded.

"How about 12.15 p.m. next Wednesday?" asked Lord Camoys.

"Fine," I said.

"See you then. Goodbye."

Obviously, especially as I had never met Lord Camoys, the owner of Stonor Park at Henley-on-Thames and the eldest member of a distinguished and ancient recusant family, I wondered what he wanted from me.

The following Wednesday I arrived at Boodle's and was approached by a dark-set middle-aged man who immediately introduced himself as Camoys and asked whether I would like a drink. Feeling very much in need of Dutch courage, I said that I would like a large gin and tonic. Once I had this in my hand, Lord Camoys suggested to me that we should go into the dining room. From the moment we sat down, he began to interrogate me. There is no other word for it.

"What do you think of the Pope? What about papal infallibility? Do you believe in the Virgin Birth? And where do you stand on contraception?" he asked.

What Lord Camoys probably never appreciated was that by now I was accustomed to undergraduates asking these questions and more almost daily, so I was not unduly disturbed. What I couldn't work out, however, was why he asked these questions and did not engage in any other type of conversation. At the end of lunch I thanked him and left without being any the wiser as to why he had invited me to Boodle's.

The following week I received another unusual phone call, only this time from a Catholic housemaster at Eton College, called Michael Atkinson, inviting me to dinner. Never having either seen or been to Eton, I accepted.

Present at the dinner table was the welcoming housemaster's elderly mother, clearly a strong-minded lady from the north, who, like Camoys though more thoroughly, put me through my paces to determine whether or not I held orthodox Catholic views. (It was at that dinner, incidentally, that I learnt that Lord Camoys was the president of the Catholic parents' society at Eton.)

A week later I received a letter from the head master of Eton inviting me to come and see him. By now I was beginning to suspect a plot. I could not help asking myself whether I was being headhunted. In his study a few days later I was soon to discover the answer.

John Lewis, the head master at Eton at the time, had asked to see me in order to make me an offer. He wanted to know if I would come to Eton as the resident Catholic chaplain and a teacher of history and religion at the start of the next academic year when my contract at

Oxford would have ended. After consulting my bishop, I accepted his offer and could not help wondering what my priestly vocation had in store for me next.

On arriving at Eton in September 1996 I discovered that, rather like the ancient universities of Oxford and Cambridge, Eton is scattered in and around a town. One could be forgiven for wondering where the town ends and the school starts. There is no obvious clue from the buildings; few stand out from one another on account of their size, beauty or age. There are exceptions, but to see these one is obliged to search, especially within what is known as school yard or the area that houses the oldest college buildings, such as the college chapel, library, dining room, cloisters, a seventeenth-century classroom known as Upper School and a fifteenth-century classroom known as Lower School.

It's the same with Eton's inhabitants. Boys and masters, or "beaks" as these latter are most frequently called, are to be found living all over the town, not confined to one area. Many of its 166 beaks live above the town's shops or frequent its pubs. Boys live in twenty-four different houses each comprising fifty boys, plus the college of seventy scholars, each with a housemaster and a dame or house matron. Boys can be seen at any time in the town's street, on their way to classes, at the school's tuck shop, in chapel, on the school's playing fields or crossing the bridge that divides Eton proper from Windsor. This proximity of school and town is because the founder of the school, King Henry VI, an ineffectual but saintly monarch, who ended his days by being murdered in the Tower of London, deliberately chose to establish his school within sight and reach of the court at Windsor Castle. He placed it where for centuries kings had stabled their horses, in the small extension of Windsor called Eton, across the River Thames.

Henry VI founded the college in 1440 for seventy poor scholars. He was a deeply religious man and, besides establishing a Catholic pilgrimage centre at Eton dedicated to the Virgin Mary, his aim was to provide himself with an educated civil service. From Eton it was hoped that the scholars would go on to university (Henry also founded King's College, Cambridge, for this purpose), and ultimately become the nucleus of an educated body of men at the service of their king and country. Although the religious purpose of Eton disappeared at the Reformation, the school remained.

After Eton was founded it was not long before aristocrats and courtiers requested the king to allow their sons to be educated alongside the seventy scholars – a request the king agreed to on condition that such pupils would lodge outside the college in boarding houses in the town and be known as "Oppidans". This practice of King's Scholars and Oppidans living separate lives but being educated together persists to this day, even though the school now numbers almost 1,300.

Over the centuries the notion that Eton is an establishment for an exclusive elite has become one of the ideas most associated with the school. This image persists and is buttressed by the fact that both Prince William and Prince Harry are Old Etonians, not to mention the Conservative Party leader, David Cameron, and the Mayor of London, Boris Johnson. However, whereas in former times the school may have been the formative environment of some nineteen prime ministers – ranging from the first, Robert Walpole, to such as Gladstone and Harold Macmillan – and poets such as Shelley and writers such as George Orwell, generals such as Wellington and explorers such as Wilfred Thesiger, today the offspring of the aristocracy have largely been displaced by the sons of city merchants and bankers, lawyers, editors of newspapers, and those who work in the media. There are, of course, in the school sons of those who still contrive to manage largely inherited family estates in the country, but these are a dwindling minority, as they are throughout the nation at large.

After attending university many present-day Etonians choose to pursue careers in the City. Whereas in pre-World War II days their goal may have been to serve their country either throughout the British empire or in other concrete ways by becoming MPs, lawyers, doctors, teachers or entering other professions such as the Foreign Office, Civil Service and armed services, today those who follow this sort of career are in a minority. For at least two decades in recent times, increasing numbers of Etonians have been choosing to enter the leisure industries, such as the theatre, the art world, writing and journalism, television and the world of high technology. The frequent aim of the majority of Etonians, at the start of their careers at least, is to acquire money.

Whereas many Etonians may come from affluent backgrounds, the wish of the founder to provide an education for the less well off has not been forgotten. The seventy scholarships begun by King Henry still exist, and many other kinds of scholarships, bursaries and grants or exhibitions are available and distributed to a larger number of pupils from overseas and at home than is often realised.

Although I came to love the school enormously, its history, cultural opportunities, high standards and especially its academic excellence, I did wonder from the very beginning how much the influence of religion, practically speaking, pervaded its day-to-day proceedings. At the time of my appointment more than a few of my fellow priests criticised me for taking on the post at Eton. Why, they wanted to know, had I chosen to work among what they called part of the Establishment? Why had I decided to become a chaplain in a non-Catholic school? Why had I chosen to work among the rich? Similar questions were asked of me by some of the head teachers of prominent Catholic public schools, one of whom actually attacked my appointment in *The Times*.

What they all failed to realise was that, though many Etonians had money, this did not always mean that they were actually rich in more important ways. Beneath the cover of affluence I was soon to discover how many of them came from divorced and dysfunctional families, how many lacked emotional support, and how many were sent to boarding school simply because it was a family tradition or because their parents could not be bothered to have them at home. The pastoral opportunities at Eton were therefore immense.

What many Catholic head teachers utterly failed to take into account was that Eton had immediate access to the M4, M3 and M25 motorways, was less than an hour from central London, and only twenty-five minutes from Heathrow. These were all positive inducements for parents to send their sons to Eton. Excellent road communications enabled many parents to visit the school on Saturdays to watch their sons on the playing fields and to collect them for lunch at home on Sundays. In any event, in the evening of the day that my appointment was criticised in *The Times*, I received a telephone call from Cardinal Hume in which he told me to take no notice and to get on with the job.

As head master, Lewis was a deceptively shy, private and sometimes awkward man. He was also a gentle man, except when roused. Socialising did not come easy either to him or his Danish-born wife, Vibeke. She had keen artistic tastes, was generous and possessed a valuable sense of humour. It would, however, have been a mistake to interpret Lewis' shyness as meaning he did not have strong and definite views, but he was also a highly analytical thinker. As so often is the case, this combination of qualities meant that he saw too many sides to any question and was notoriously slow in coming to decisions.

Lewis was also a believing and practising Christian at a time when the majority of beaks were indifferent to religion and preferred to attend chapel only when duty called. Only occasionally in my experience did Lewis betray what might be termed sectarian prejudice and blatant preference for the established Church of England. When this occurred, however, it took the form of failing totally to understand the liturgical needs of the two hundred Roman Catholic boys and their desire for a decent place of worship. Only under his successor did the sizeable Catholic minority finally obtain permission to worship in one of the school's two chapels.

The fact that Lewis was a practising Christian meant that he was genuinely open to discussion when a boy came before him on a matter of discipline. Behind the scenes he was also concerned for any boy who was seriously ill, a matter another head might have left to the boy's housemaster.

Having taught in schools before, I had no qualms about teaching at Eton. I did wonder, however, whether Etonians would be any different from other boys of the same age. I already knew from past experience that a teacher should begin by exercising firm control in a classroom and only gradually over time loosen the reins. I assumed that, because admission to Eton is not easy, those I was about to meet would be intelligent and bright. I also guessed that at this first meeting they would attempt to weigh me up, see if I was strict or lenient, and most of all if I was possessed of a sense of humour. I knew that one of their worst fears would be that my lessons would be boring.

Nevertheless my first encounter with a typical group of Etonians still remains fresh in my memory. It not only immediately took on the form of a steep learning experience for me and one that I actually relished, but it made clear to me why many people regard Etonians as arrogant.

Sitting in a classroom on my first day, I was gathering my thoughts and waiting for the class to arrive. This particular class were all thirteen-year-olds and all newcomers to the school. They were intelligent, fresh from first-class preparatory schools and, as such, as bright as buttons if not precocious. As they arrived and drifted towards their desks, three boys stopped in front of my desk and started a conversation as young boys do. Then very quickly I became aware that the first boy of the three was staring hard at me.

Without hesitation he said, "Sir, you're really old, aren't you? I mean really old."

Before I could respond, the second boy then said, "You're also rather short, aren't you, Sir?"

Enough of this, I thought, and replied rather proudly, "Listen you, where I come from we measure from the chin up, in other words we take note of the size of one's brain, not one's bulk."

And then, quick as a flash, and with an *adopted* air of total innocence, he replied, "Which chin are we talking about, Sir?"

Fortunately, seeing the funny side of this and admiring the boy's nerve, I grinned.

Nevertheless the third boy, affecting to take pity on me, now joined in, "Don't take any notice of them, Sir. They're just rude. If I had as few years left as you, I would live life to the full. Get the most of the little that's left."

On this occasion I decided to say no more than to point out to everyone, in no uncertain terms, that there was a line over which from then on they should not tread, unless they wished to face immediate retribution. I added that in my class they should never speak without permission, and for good measure I ordered them to sit down and to shut up. I had already decided to wait, no matter how long it took, for the occasion (and I was sure it would come) when I would turn the tables on this gang of three.

Sure enough, five years later, when all three were in their last term at school, the occasion came when I was asked to address all two hundred members of the Upper Sixth who were shortly to leave Eton for good, including them. By then the three were genuine friends of mine. They had grown into three sophisticated and charming so-called gentlemen, without losing their cheekiness. In many important ways they hadn't changed, so I decided to employ the ancient technique of storytelling, the rule of three, and treat them to their own medicine.

I began my talk by telling the assembled gathering of my first encounter with these three particular Etonians, saying that I couldn't obviously single them out or name them, but I did want to speak about each of them in turn. Now it so happened that the boy who had once described me as being very old was now a member of Pop, in other words he was a prefect.

There were only twenty or so prefects in the whole school of 1,300 boys, so it was something of a real ambition among the boys to be elected to Pop. Those who were in it were not only highly privileged but were free to wear a different uniform from the rest of the school, including colourful waistcoats, so they thought themselves rather awesome and special. Prince William, incidentally, who later became a member of Pop, at one time sported a waistcoat designed like a Union Jack.

I informed the gathering about the first of the three boys I was talking about, that I had been informed by his best friend that he actually possessed seventeen waistcoats and that, even before being elected to Pop, he had practised his walk, or rather distinctive swagger, for hours in front of a mirror. I said that he was nowadays a wonder to behold and he reminded me of a peacock, except that he had swollen in size while in Pop, and had become somewhat rotund in shape.

By now everyone was looking around trying to identify the prefect I was talking about, which wasn't difficult because he was on duty at the time and sitting in a specially raised pew to overlook the assembly, and he had gone bright red. I added that, even though he was bound for Oxford, he would never again have such a stage as now on which to parade himself.

I went on to tell everyone that the second boy (the one who had referred to my lack of height) was now a member of what was called Sixth Form Select, a group of about twenty of the cleverest boys in the school, chosen for their high intelligence. I said he was so tall and thin, he could be compared to a "brain on a stalk". Everyone knew who I was talking about and turned to see how the boy was taking it.

I then informed the assembled gathering that the third boy (the one who had told me to live life to the full) had caused me to start going bald with worry. I said I seemed to have spent the past five years trying to keep him out of trouble, on the straight and narrow, and several times had begged the head master not to expel him. He was always in trouble of one kind or another. At which point the boy in question, nicknamed the Chief, to no one's surprise was clearly keen to stand up and take a bow.

During my time at Eton what struck me most, especially in the relationships that existed between beaks and boys, was the emphasis placed on developing a boy's potential. Among the most dedicated beaks there seemed to be a common acceptance of the dictum that we should all enable every individual we teach to realise all his potentialities in every way possible. This was an idea that I had personally embraced from the time when I had first begun teaching in 1958. Even so, since my conversion to Catholicism, I considered that this idea was insufficient by itself and that it needed to be enfolded within a larger framework of specific duties and responsibilities towards others, and preferably that framework should be specifically Christian.

This notion of training everyone to realise his potential was vividly and especially illustrated in the case of an Etonian who was later to become the well-known biographer Hugo Vickers, but his story could have been repeated endlessly in different ways in the case of hundreds of other boys.

When he first arrived at Eton from his prep school, it was discovered that Hugo Vickers had no talent for games, in fact he was not only hopeless at games but utterly uncoordinated. It was as though the very thought of games made him ill. Fortunately Hugo Vickers had a wise housemaster who, possibly at the end of his tether, asked him what he was most interested in and Vickers replied, "Windsor Castle".

"From now on," said his housemaster, "every time we have games you will go to Windsor Castle, and on your return you will tell me what you have learnt." And so he did.

Five years later, by the time Vickers was in the Upper Sixth, he knew all the staff at Windsor Castle. It didn't matter whether they worked in the kitchens, were cleaners, guides, gardeners and so on, he knew them all to the highest-ranking officers in the Guards. He could have told you the castle's history from Norman times to the present, the different architectural styles of the various buildings, the paintings and furniture each room contained and how the castle is administered.

Soon after leaving school he was writing biographies of the kings and queens who had lived in Windsor Castle and today he is acknowledged as a world authority and expert on it. Whenever someone is needed on radio or television to comment on the royal family, Vickers is called upon. Presumably if you were to ask him what was the turning point in his young life, he would say when his housemaster ordered him to go to Windsor Castle whenever the house was playing games.

At Eton all the concentration of talent, resources and opportunities for learning and engaging in extracurricular activities means, however, that the boys are under enormous and constant pressure to succeed. As one Old Etonian, David Thomas, observed in an article in *The Independent* newspaper in May 2000, "The biggest single error made by Eton's ideological opponents is to presume that the school is a strawberry-swilling paradise for indolent toffs. Wrong. It is relentlessly competitive in every aspect of its activities. Boys are listed, graded and ranked against one another all the time. They compete for everything and are expected to win."

As the Catholic chaplain at Eton this policy of fostering and developing a pupil's potential was one that came almost automatically to me, albeit with the reservations I have already mentioned, but another was not so common among beaks. This was that of protecting and indeed encouraging boys who did not fit easily into the Eton system, more than a few of whom often found themselves in trouble with the school authorities. When challenged by other beaks as to why I did this, I would reply that, just as it was the sick not the healthy who needed a doctor, and just as Jesus felt it necessary to seek out sinners, so did I in my role as a priest.

The result was that during the next eight years I metaphorically beat a path to the head master's study whenever a boy came to me in serious trouble. In the head master's study I would plead the boy's case, explain the background to his situation, or even seek a reversal of the decision to expel him. Knowing the home background of so many of the boys, I gave this work priority because of its pastoral nature. This, however, could have unexpected repercussions.

The proximity of Eton to the royal court at Windsor meant that Etonians were accustomed to events involving royalty and also to the occasional visit to the school from different members of the royal family. This had been the case down all the centuries since the school had been founded by Henry VI in 1440. It came as no surprise to me therefore in 1997 when the Provost at that time enquired whether I would like to meet the Queen Mother.

On the day in question I was duly introduced to her and should have known that the meeting would contain some surprises.

"I hear [pronounced *hair*] that you have been at Eton a year [pronounced *yah*], Fr Forrester," said Her Majesty.

"Yes, Ma'am," I quietly replied.

"But what is a yah in the life of Eton?" she asked.

Somewhat taken aback, I didn't know how to respond to this, though I was sorely tempted to ask the Queen Mother, "What is a year in the life of a nonagenarian?"

Then there was a deafening silence, which protocol required should not be broken until the Queen Mother decided to speak again. It went on so long, however, that I took the initiative.

"You know, Ma'am, the boy who was carrying your train at the Garter ceremony last week?" I said.

"Yas," came the reply.

"Well, he is one of mine. I teach him history," I lamely said.

"I think he is a good boy," said the Queen Mother.

This remark threw me completely because the Etonian in question, the younger son of an Earl, was one of those boys frequently in trouble for breaking school rules and whose cause I had more than once had to plead before the head master. To hear him described as a "good" boy had simply made my jaw drop and I wanted desperately to laugh.

The Queen Mother, without hesitation, said, "I only said I *thought* he was a good boy." And, with a twinkle in her eye, she departed.

Each year it was part of my duty to prepare Catholic boys for confirmation. As part of this it was my custom to give them a talk on adolescence, informing them that I considered a statement that had appeared in the media to be way off the mark. This was that teenagers were moody, rebellious and never serious. I described this as a gigantic myth and a nonsensical generalisation, probably made by someone who had forgotten his or her own life between the ages of twelve and eighteen. I also told them that another myth was the extent of sexual activity and drug habits among adolescents, even though we all knew young people who were layabouts, binge drinkers, and into drugs and sex.

Throughout the preparation for confirmation I would emphasise that Jesus was a complete human being, and like us in all things except sin, so everything about who they were, and what stage of their development they had reached, he understood. Then I would give a rundown on the physical, mental and spiritual characteristics of adolescence, followed by a discussion as to how and why they were developing their own identity, experiencing an increase in conflict with those in authority, undergoing peer pressure, and how they would henceforth be engaged in a search for understanding and relations with the opposite sex.

Occasionally I would be asked to address the parents of the Catholic boys on how they might relate with their adolescent sons, with illustrations on how Jesus related with people. I would ask them to examine the Gospels and observe how Jesus accompanied people on their "journey" through life, and I would suggest that as parents they should walk alongside their sons to maturity while adopting deliberate techniques. These techniques had in fact become my own guiding principles in dealing with my pupils and were as follows:

1. Win their trust by truly listening. Try to hear what they are *not* saying. (This involves not being judgemental.)

2. Show real interest in what they say and are doing. (This does not mean necessarily agreeing with their views or behaviour.)

3. Refuse to be shocked by anything they say or claim to believe. (Appreciate you may be being used as a testing or sounding board.)

4. Be available at all times and patient. (This should indicate to them that they are important and of value.)

5. See each as an individual with their own gifts and weaknesses, made in the image of God.

6. Take meals with them and encourage them to relax and be open. (Note how often in the Gospels Jesus shares a meal with people.)

7. Challenge them as Jesus challenged the rich young man in the Gospels.

8. Discover their interests and spend time with them, for example by going with them to the theatre, cinema, sporting activities, football matches, concerts and art galleries.

9. Be aware of the value of humour and laughter as instruments of discovery as to who they are.

10. Avoid being inquisitorial.

11. Share with them the story of your own path to adulthood.

12. When the opportunity arises, make clear that Jesus himself spent a great deal of time actually explaining his purpose to his disciples (Similarly they must indicate what their faith is based on.)

13. By their practice of the faith indicate to young people the importance and place in their lives of prayer and worship. Stress that without prayer and the sacraments a Christian's life would be considerably diminished.

I would add that only when trust is genuinely won would adolescents truly open up concerning their needs, urges, hopes and fears, in other words reveal their real selves behind their adopted masks. Furthermore a golden rule for adults was always to be themselves when dealing with adolescents, and never to pretend. I would say that adolescents are rarely fooled, they loathe hypocrisy, would watch one closely (especially those who have been hurt in the past) and test a parent's ability not to betray their confidences.

Finally, a thread that should run through all their exchanges with adolescents and young adults should be the (often unspoken) presence of Christ. His teaching and love should be implicit in everything said and done with them.

My own relations with my Etonian pupils, however, were often not without their amusing side. On one occasion I was invited to preach at the wedding of a former student from Oxford who had once lived at the chaplaincy. Both he and his future wife were Anglicans so the ceremony was to take place in the bride's local Anglican parish church and to be conducted by the vicar.

On the day in question I arrived at the church only to discover that the vicar was a woman. To tell the truth I had never previously met a woman vicar, but to my astonishment we got on like a house on fire from the word go. This was probably because I was on my best behaviour, she had a delightful sense of humour, and I quickly had to banish from my mind all images of the Vicar of Dibley.

The following week the vicar invited me to dinner with her family at her house and I accepted. I accepted largely because, by then, I knew that the vicar was bringing up three children on her own and I wanted somehow to help.

Before we sat down for dinner, I had been advised by the vicar that the second daughter would be late home from sixth-form college, and as we waited we exchanged stories, laughed at jokes and generally enjoyed ourselves. Then suddenly, with a loud bang, the door burst open and into the room came the second daughter, who was seventeen. She was wearing huge round earrings, a bare midriff, had a jewel in her navel and another in her nose, and was chewing fiercely on a piece of gum! I tried not to look astonished. Without further ado, she then came straight up to me and asked if I would do her a favour. How was I to respond? I looked at the vicar, who was smiling, and agreed.

Then she said – and her very words were – "Fr Forrester, would you fix me up with an Etonian?"

"What sort of Etonian?" I enquired, somewhat surprised.

"One who is my age or older, fit [meaning good looking] and intelligent," she said.

I took a deep breath, held out my arm and asked, "Do you have a mobile? Because if you do, write its number here on my wrist."

After she had done so, I said, "You'll hear from an Etonian, such as you have described, within the next three days."

On returning to Eton I collared a sixth-former called Sam, who had all the qualities she had specified. I asked him to ring the number on my wrist and arrange to meet the girl. He was quite eager to do so and went off happily grinning like the proverbial Cheshire cat.

When I next bumped into Sam, I enquired whether he had done what I asked. "Oh, yes, Sir, of course," he replied.

"And what happened?" I asked.

"I took her out," said Sam.

"And then?"

"Oh, I dumped her," he said.

"Why?"

"Because I couldn't get a word in edgeways," he replied with a perfectly straight face.

Incidentally, Sam subsequently went up to Oxford and obtained a first. He is now something in the City.

Another memorable experience I had at Eton, but of a quite different kind, occurred when I was sitting one morning in my flat in Eton and the telephone rang. It was a call from a good friend of mine informing me that her mother had died.

"I am so sorry," I replied, "is there any way in which I can help?"

"As you know," she said, "I am a convert to Islam. My husband and children are all Muslims. We are worried about the funeral and you're the only Christian priest we know. My mother was a Scottish Presbyterian."

"I don't wish to be insensitive," I said, "but do you wish to bury or cremate your mother's body?"

"Oh, cremate," my friend replied.

"Then it's easy," I said, "book a crematorium and I will do it."

The following Saturday I arrived at the crematorium in London and immediately noticed that the majority of the congregation were Muslim Arabs from all over the Middle East who had come to support the family.

"Father, Father," I heard someone shout, "I am the organist, I am Jewish."

"Shush!" I whispered. "Almost everyone here is Arab."

"Sorry," he responded. "But I do want you to meet my wife. She's German. Her parents were Nazis and in favour of killing all Jews!"

"Shush!" I said again.

"By the way," the organist went on unabashedly, "the choir are all black, Protestant, hot Gospel singers from Jamaica!"

During the first hymn I reflected how unusual the service was becoming: the woman in the coffin was Scottish Presbyterian; the congregation were virtually all Muslims from Egypt, Saudi Arabia, Syria and Lebanon; the organist was Jewish; the choir were evangelical Protestants; and the priest, in other words myself, was Roman Catholic. But all this was nothing to my surprise when we reached the sermon.

I had decided to quote the Koran on the resurrection of the dead, but no one had told me how Muslims react when one quotes the Koran. I began reading and every time I paused the congregation responded with shouts of "Allahu Akbar" and the waving of arms. In my surprise I wondered whether they were friends or foes. I didn't know then that what they were shouting was "God is great!"

After it was all over I reflected on this unusual experience. It was the most remarkable funeral I've ever conducted. It also made me think seriously about inter-faith relations. What a pity, I thought, that we, of all different religions, could only come together because of a death. I considered this particularly sad because, as early as 1986, the Pope had said, "the challenge of peace in the world transcends all religions".

I remembered that, after the events of 11th September 2001, both the Pope and the Archbishop of Canterbury had made a point of meeting with other world religious leaders and both had particularly stressed how much the three monotheistic religions Judaism, Christianity and Islam had in common, especially concerning the resurrection of the dead. Surely, I thought, it was high time we did some unlearning, in the sense of getting rid of our prejudices, our stereotypical notions and our sectarian behaviour in relation to other religions or denominations. For justification for this attitude, I told myself that we only had to look to Northern Ireland (Catholics versus Protestants), to Israel and Palestine (Jews and Arabs), or to India (Muslims and Hindus) to see what harm had been done in the name of religion.

It was for this reason that, throughout my years at Eton, I strove to argue that in our now global and fragile world we could no longer afford to remain enclosed in mental, emotional and spiritual bunkers, unless we wished to become fossils. Instead we needed much more to reach out to the hearts, souls and intellects of those who believe and worship differently from ourselves, but who equally are made in the image of God, especially to the two million Muslims in Britain.

I was fond of reminding the boys at Eton that Pope John Paul II, speaking to Jewish and Muslim leaders in Jerusalem on his last visit there in March 2000, had said: "What is demanded of all of us is that, holding to what we believe, we listen respectfully to one another, seek to discern all that is good and holy in each other's teachings, and cooperate in supporting everything that favours mutual understanding and peace."

Throughout my eight years at Eton I often thought that I had never been happier. There was one thought, however, which troubled me the whole time I was there and which was only partly resolved once I had left and began to look back on my time there. This was what appeared to me to be an absence of an overall or overarching *raison d'être* to life at Eton. What was the philosophy underpinning all the activities, both mental and physical, that took place there? Was there even a hint of a spiritual explanation? What would the founder, Henry VI, think of today's Eton?

It did not seem sufficient to me to justify Eton's existence by emphasising the irrefutably excellent quality of its education and in particular the quality of the teaching that took place within it. Neither did it seem enough to point to the school's amazing facilities, sporting and otherwise. Nor was it totally convincing, though true, to expatiate about how many leaders in every branch of society and down the ages had come from Eton. What I sought and never found was something akin to the original religious reason of Henry VI for founding Eton: a spiritual explanation and justification for its continuing existence, which would be something more than just a defence of its liberal values and modus vivendi. Its absence struck me as a weakness, similar to something I had detected about Oxford when I was there.

Virtually every day I was there I attended or led morning prayers in the college chapel. I considered it one of the most beautiful and historic buildings in England, both architecturally and in its ambience. Not once did I ever lose my sense of wonder at the thought of the large number of Etonians who had sat or knelt there down the centuries and had gone on to unimaginable heights of greatness in the life of the nation. The quality of the choral singing and organ playing was unrivalled and the daily readings from the King James Bible never failed to move one. But there was always this nagging thought. Were we actually engaged in worship or simply enjoying a huge aesthetic experience celebrating the achievements of Eton? There was no question about what the purpose of the founder, Henry VI, had been in building such a magnificent chapel. These were the kind of doubts that had bedevilled the Old Etonian Monsignor Ronald Knox about his time at the school and which he described in his book *A Spiritual Aeneid*. Only later did I reach some kind of peace of mind on this matter of worship, when I explored how people discover God in different ways and how some especially find God through the medium of art and music. However, to the question of what Eton stands for in the eternal order of things I never found a satisfactory answer, which was something that made me sad.

8

A priest in residence

In 2004 I turned seventy and thought it high time I left Eton to make way for a younger man after eight wonderful years. With considerable sadness, therefore, I took my departure from the school at the end of June that year with the immediate plan of flying to Bolivia in South America for a stay of three weeks to visit a young newly ordained priest that I had met the year before in England. It was to be my first experience of poverty on a large scale, Bolivia being the poorest country in South America.

It was in Bolivia that I also met and stayed with an extraordinary man, the Archbishop of Cochabamba, Tito Solari. He is an Italian and, many years before, he had been sent as a missionary priest by his superiors to Bolivia. When he first arrived he too had been greatly shocked by the poverty and primitive conditions in which so many of his parishioners lived. Some years later he was made an archbishop. By that time, however, he had adopted a way of life which he continued and still today continues to pursue, even though he now has huge responsibilities and many more people to serve. He shares the lifestyle of his people.

Instead of a large house, he continues to live in a modest building with a tin roof, with only cold running water (sometimes no water at all), and none of the facilities we usually take for granted. He does not own a car, but travels around his diocese by bus. He wears simple clothes, eats simple food and is available at all times to people in need. He never turns anyone away from his door.

Such is the people's trust in him that he is often called upon to act as an arbiter in disputes affecting their livelihood. Some years ago, for example, and before recent government legislation, the city's water supply was privatised and sold to a consortium of international companies who immediately doubled or tripled the water rates. In what became known as *la guerra del agua*, the war of water, thousands of citizens demonstrated in the streets, resulting in armed troops being called in, arrests being made, one protester being killed and injuries being inflicted on many others. The crisis was only solved when the archbishop persuaded both the water companies to back down and lower their prices, and the protesters to disperse.

Archbishop Solari is also renowned for his personal acts of charity. On one occasion, for example, he personally paid for the medical treatment of a young thief set on fire by an angry mob when caught in the very act of stealing. At the same time as the archbishop rebuked those responsible for inflicting third-degree burns on the young man, he also berated the police for not providing adequate security against such criminal acts as theft.

The people love him. Whilst they never forget that he is an archbishop, they are never overawed or frightened to approach him. They recognise that he cares for them. They see in him the kind of disciple spoken of by Jesus in the Gospel: someone like himself who "came not to be served but to serve".

Earlier that year and before going to Bolivia, I had visited Woldingham, an independent boarding and day school for girls, to say Mass for the girls at the request of the lay chaplain, Elsie Sebastian, the member of the Teresian Society who had once been my assistant at the Oxford chaplaincy. After the Mass the charismatic, tall, attractive and energetic headmistress of Woldingham Girls' School in Surrey, Diana Vernon, a person of considerable elan, approached me, clearly with a plan in her mind.

Towering over me, she began by asking, "Fr Forrester, what do you intend doing when you leave Eton?"

Wondering why she wanted to know, I vaguely replied, "I intend going to the Lake District to write books."

109

Without stopping, she then asked, "Why don't you come here and do that?"

This was an attractive suggestion. Woldingham is situated in a beautiful wooded valley three miles long, formerly the site of a stately home, once lived in by William Wilberforce. The whole valley of seven hundred acres, together with the stately home, was bought by the Sacred Heart nuns shortly after the Second World War and turned into a school. It is also the home of deer, foxes, badgers, rabbits and many different kinds of bird. Besides the school, the valley also contains a farm and a railway station, with trains to London every half-hour, the journey taking just thirty-five minutes.

Nevertheless I hesitated. I wondered what was involved in the headmistress's suggestion. On receiving no immediate answer from me, she continued: "We'll give you a house. We will gut it and refurbish it according to your wishes and we will pay all your bills – water, electricity, council tax and so on. All except your phone bill." (My phone bill was, in fact, my biggest bill.)

That is quite an offer, I thought, but still did not respond.

"We'll give you all your meals, lunch and supper every day, including during the school holidays."

Wow, I thought, this woman is really keen to have me at the school; but I still hesitated.

"We'll pay you," she then said.

To which I immediately replied, "I'll come."

In return for all these generous provisions, I learnt that I would be called the priest in residence and my duties were to say Mass for the girls on Wednesdays, Sundays and holy days of obligation, to administer the sacrament of reconciliation, to take a school assembly for the staff and girls on Thursdays, to assist the lay chaplain to prepare girls for confirmation, and to give occasional talks to sixth-formers.

Woldingham School owes its existence to a remarkable French woman called St Madeleine Sophie Barat. During her life she founded one hundred and five convents or schools in twelve different countries. Woldingham grew from the one she established in England in 1842.

For anyone – even someone hostile to religion – who examines the life of Madeleine Sophie, the verdict must be that she was an extraordinary woman. She was born in 1779, ten years before the French Revolution of 1789, which brought the abolition of the monarchy, upheaval, turmoil and monumental changes to France; and not only to France, but to the whole of Europe. In 1793–94 there occurred the so-called Reign of Terror, when thousands were executed on the guillotine. During this time her brother, Louis, experienced two years' imprisonment. In its turn the Reign of Terror was succeeded by the dictatorship and wars of Napoleon. This was the world in which Madeleine Sophie grew up and in which, no matter what, she was determined to hold on to and maintain her Catholic faith.

When fully grown, Madeleine Sophie Barat was only 4 feet 10 inches in height, with brown eyes and brown hair. By the age of twelve she was helping her mother through a depression and also running the family business. As an adolescent she was described as impatient, impulsive and energetic, but no one could doubt her ability.

Her brother Louis (who was also her godfather) took her education seriously and taught her himself at home. He taught her Latin, Greek, history, the natural sciences, Spanish and Italian. She read the classics in their original languages. A few years later in Paris he taught her theology, biblical studies, the Church Fathers and mathematics.

Very early on, Madeleine Sophie expressed the wish to become an enclosed Carmelite nun, but the circumstances of the time prevented this. However, she never lost her desire to engage in contemplative prayer and throughout her whole life grasped opportunities to spend time with God in prayer. When she was only twenty-one she founded the Society of the Sacred Heart, today a global order of nuns.

For decades she administered the finances of the expanding Society of the Sacred Heart with facility and skill. She travelled incessantly for over forty years all over Europe, visiting schools and convents. She negotiated complicated agreements with authorities in both Church and State. She was a builder, an educator and a spiritual guide. She was highly thought of by popes and princes. Nevertheless one of her major concerns was to bring the Gospel of Christ into the lives of the hundreds of girls and nuns in her schools.

By the time of her death in 1865 she had become an inspirational example and patron for women everywhere, especially for anyone seeking how to lead a Christian life in a non-Christian world. From the start I could not help wondering whether Woldingham School would live up to the high Catholic standards set by Madeleine Sophie Barat.

What slightly concerned me from the beginning was the proportion of Catholic pupils in the school in relation to others. Of the five hundred or so girls, there was a significantly greater number of Anglicans, and girls of no Christian adherence whatsoever, than of Catholics. Diana Vernon, the headmistress, was herself a committed Anglican, and only a minority of the staff were practising Catholics. This is not an unusual state of affairs these days in Catholic independent schools and is largely due to financial factors. In order simply to survive, it has become necessary for them to admit pupils of different faiths or none. For the same reason many of them also encourage overseas students to seek admittance, particularly from Asia.

At Woldingham, the only major religious requirement of all pupils, whatever their faith, was that they should attend Mass on Sundays. (On major feast days, with the approval of the Catholic Bishop of Arundel and Brighton, an Anglican priest would be present at Mass and distribute Holy Communion, already consecrated in his local parish, to girls who were not Catholics.) The fact that Catholics were in a minority in the school, however, meant that it was extremely difficult to maintain a Catholic ethos in the school, and ordinary Catholic practices, such as saying the rosary and the Stations of the Cross or devotion to the saints, were largely absent.

Several years before, the Sisters of the Sacred Heart had also withdrawn from teaching at the school and had handed over the running of the school to an essentially lay board of governors. This was due, as in most religious orders in Europe and the West, to the enormous drop in religious vocations. The only nuns still at Woldingham were an assistant head in charge of pastoral affairs, not a Sister of the Sacred

Heart but a Sister of Mercy, who could not have been more devoted to the care of the girls and who was later to become a headmistress herself elsewhere, and two remarkable retired Sacred Heart Sisters who had chosen to remain in the valley. These latter were among my chief friends and spiritual supports during my time at the school.

Although as far back as 1972 in Southampton I had experience of working in a girls' school, the contrast with Eton and the teaching of boys was enormous. It took me some time to become acclimatised to this fact. Nevertheless I was delighted to observe that girls were often more spontaneously kind, creative and caring than boys, not least during the annual dinners that I organised for eighteen sixth-formers from Eton with the eighteen prefects at Woldingham. I also agreed to become the personal tutor to several girls and did what I could, often by simply being there, to assist them to negotiate the rapids of adolescence and sort out their problems with their parents.

Among the many discussions I had with the girls of Woldingham who were my personal pupils was the question of what they intended to do with their lives when they left. Together we reflected that, one hundred years ago, if one were to ask an average teenage girl in Great Britain what she intended to do on leaving school, her choice was very limited. Most girls one hundred years ago would simply hope to marry and have children.

We agreed that a small minority of girls a century ago might try to go to university, some might become suffragettes and campaign for women to be given the vote, but unless the young women had money of their own, opportunities for them one hundred years ago were extremely limited. My pupils were disturbed by the fact that it was then thought that a woman's place was in the home and often she was regarded literally as the property of her husband, in the manner sometimes found in a Galsworthy novel.

When we discussed by contrast the many openings available to them, they discovered that the opportunities were vast, though in some areas still not equal to those available to men. After university more than a few of the girls would say they intended to do something in the City in order to make money. This was because the ethos of the society we now live in is one in which a major aim is to acquire and to consume.

It was true that more than a few of the girls said they would try to do something useful in their gap years, between school and university, and work in underdeveloped countries. And there still remained a minority who would seek to serve others throughout their lives. This was chiefly because they were concerned about the great issues of our time, such as racism, peace, human rights, poverty and climate change.

Of course others said they would seek to enter the professions, to become nurses, doctors, lawyers, teachers and so on, or increasingly they would enter creative occupations in the world of the arts, leisure activities and entertainment. But I was left in no doubt as to their enthusiasm to do something valuable with their lives once they left. One girl in particular remains in my mind for the fact that she summed up her ambition by quoting lines based on words sometimes attributed to Robert Louis Stevenson:

That person is a success who has lived well, laughed often, and loved much;
Who has gained the respect of intelligent people and the love of children;
Who has filled her niche and accomplished her task;
Who leaves the world better than she found it, whether by an improved poppy, a perfect poem or a rescued soul;
Who never lacked appreciation of Earth's beauty, or failed to express it;
Who looked for the best in others and gave the best she had;
Her memory is a benediction.

The subject that I was most frequently asked to speak about by sixth-formers was what happens to us after we die, and I would usually remind them that, when a former headmaster of Ampleforth was once asked, "What is the purpose of education?" he responded by saying, "To prepare pupils for death."

I would agree with them that this might sound morbid, not least because increasing numbers of people no longer believe in life after death and, with the decline in the West of the authority of the Church, such ideas as the immortality of the soul are no longer as convincing as in previous ages. But I would then explain that, for a Christian, death remains the gateway to eternal life and hopefully a life lived in the actual presence of God for ever.

Such is the scepticism of modern youth, they rarely found this convincing, but they would listen attentively and view me with eyes wide open when I would go on to say that death doesn't mean the end of everything; indeed quite the reverse. It is the beginning of true life.

I would further explain that saints call the day they die their birthday, in other words their birth into eternity. St Paul, for instance, told the people of Philippi that "My desire is to depart and be with Christ." St Ignatius of Antioch wrote to the Christians in Rome before his execution, saying, "It is better for me to die in Christ Jesus than to reign over the ends of the earth... when I shall have arrived there, then I shall be a man." So why, I would ask them, is death a modern-day taboo subject?

One of the things I enjoyed most about being at Woldingham was giving a weekly assembly to the whole school, staff and girls alike, assembled in the school's state-of-the-art theatre. In the space of eight minutes I was required to address the gathering on any subject of my own choosing. Usually I did this in the form of a PowerPoint presentation on a topic I had previously researched. These presentations could be as varied as those I gave on the history of Venice, the value and purpose of icons, globalisation, immigration, ecclesiastical buildings along the River Thames, and the insidious techniques employed by modern advertisers.

The proximity of Woldingham to London was something else that I enjoyed during my three and a half years there. It opened my eyes to just how much London has become a melting pot for people of different ethnic backgrounds and cultures. According to 2006 estimates based on the 2001 Census, in a population of 7.3 million only 4.3 million are categorised as "White British". The remainder includes people whose ethnic origins are from Asia, Africa and the Caribbean; people of mixed race; as well as Arabs, Americans, Australians and Eastern Europeans to mention just a few. London has become the most cosmopolitan and amazing city in the world. Its streets are loud with over three hundred different languages and bright with Muslim veils and beards, African robes and Caribbean dreadlocks. The recognition on my part of this diversity was also to enable me to form a friendship in a totally unexpected way.

One morning I was sitting in the school library reading the newspapers, when in came about a dozen men of all ages and sizes waiting to be interviewed for a technician's job in IT at the school. The last to enter the library was a young British Asian who was clearly a Muslim. Some weeks later I encountered this young Muslim at lunch in the staff dining room. He had succeeded in getting the job, but he confided to me across the lunch table that he had a problem. He said that it was his practice to pray five times a day but that he had nowhere to do this. It was not possible to pray in the office he shared with his colleagues and he asked me for my advice.

Without a moment's thought I reached into my pocket and handed him the keys to my house. I told him he should go there, go upstairs to the spare bedroom, and from then on use that room as a place in which to pray. He was to do so every day for the remaining time he was at Woldingham and, in the process, he and I became firm friends, exchanging ideas, discussing our different religions, and sometimes eating out together in restaurants where halal meat was available.

Each Friday he attended his local mosque. A few months after this young Muslim, in his twenties and called Abdul Sharif Rahiman, and I had first spoken, he asked me how he could become a teacher. Since he was already a university graduate, I informed him that the procedure would require him both to attend a specific university course two days a week and to obtain teaching experience in a school the rest of the week. He would be observed, given written work to complete, tested and assessed throughout this first year, and this would be followed by a second year of full-time teaching. If he were then found to be acceptable, he would become a qualified teacher.

To our delight shortly afterwards, Diana Vernon, the headmistress, informed Abdul that Woldingham would sponsor his training to become a secondary school teacher, beginning the next academic year. Throughout his time at Woldingham, Abdul became an exceptionally popular student-teacher, respected by both the girls and the staff. Today he is a highly regarded teacher in a state secondary school and I have been provided with a Muslim friend for life.

In July 2007 Diana Vernon left Woldingham to become the headmistress of the City of London School for Girls. Three months later, I decided that it was also time for me to move on and, after giving a term's notice, I left Woldingham valley for the last time in March 2008. I thought that I was to become an officially retired priest, only to discover that the word "retired" was a complete misnomer.

Epilogue

In 2008 after eighteen years away, and after filling the posts of chaplain to Oxford University, chaplain and teacher at Eton, and priest in residence at Woldingham, I finally returned to my home diocese of Portsmouth. Officially at seventy-five years of age I retired but, given the shortage of clergy, I continue to find my days frequently taken up with standing in for priests in need of a holiday or when they are ill.

Among other things, standing in for other priests naturally entails, besides saying Mass, baptising newcomers to the Church, comforting those who are bereaved, burying or cremating the dead, visiting and anointing those who are sick in hospital, officiating at weddings, preaching the word and counselling those with problems. I also find myself increasingly called upon to give talks or lectures on a variety of subjects in schools and parishes throughout the diocese. Furthermore, I have also been encouraged to take up part-time tutoring in history at the Oxford University Department of Continuing Education.

It is an absolute joy to be once again serving in a variety of different ways people of all ages and conditions. To be celebrating Mass and preaching the Gospel on Sundays to young, middle-aged and old reminds me of when I first started out as a priest and why I was ordained in 1972. Still to be teaching, lecturing and tutoring in all kinds of ways enables me to keep in touch with people of all backgrounds, ethnic groups and religions.

To be released from the burden of administrative tasks such as being responsible for parish finances and buildings, as well as from seemingly endless committee meetings of one sort or another within a parish, school, university or even diocese, is an added bonus. Such freedom enables one to concentrate on truly priestly concerns, especially being of service to others when administering the sacraments, spreading the Gospel, or simply being there for people when they are distressed or troubled.

It is this variety and the opportunity to meet and assist all different sorts of people that is definitely one of the joys of priesthood. My mother was often fond of saying in her north-country way that "we are all the same with our shirts off", to which I would usually respond by saying, "I know what you mean, mother, but we're not!" Nevertheless it is this recognition of our common humanity, and the fact that we are all made in the image of God whatever our social class, education or financial situation, that enables a priest to reach out and be of service to everyone that he encounters.

Looking back to that small boy alone on a north Devon beach at the age of nine and even further back, it is as though I have been led by a golden thread all through the length of my life. Sometimes I went off on a tangent, at other times I resisted the tug of the thread and occasionally tried to break the thread leading me altogether, but I always knew that life was more fulfilling and meaningful when I followed its direction. I now realise that this is what is meant by providence and by pursuing a vocation.

In retrospect, I have lately appreciated that what has kept me bound to the thread was prayer of the kind I first observed my mother engaged in each night as she knelt by her bed and as I was taught by Michael Hollings years ago. Prayer not in the sense of uttering many words and making demands of God but of seeking him, being aware of my need of him, enjoying his presence, listening to him and endeavouring to give him my whole attention at all times.

One of the last things that Tony Battle, my friend from our days together at the English College in Rome, asked me to do before he died was to make my priority to get to know Jesus Christ. Nowadays all else would appear secondary in my life and I am convinced that certainly no priest can survive, let alone enjoy a fulfilled life, unless he daily seeks to deepen his relationship with God through prayer and in the service of others.

In my own case I know that it is when I am consciously united to Christ that I am most happy and able simply to concentrate on the task immediately before me. I also now realise that it is God, through the workings of providence, who enabled me and continues to enable me to meet an exceptional number of unusual people, often at particular junctures in my life. I have learnt so much from such people. It seems likely that no other calling provides such opportunities and such challenges to bring the good news of Jesus Christ to so many people's daily lives. For any men or women who may wish to explore whether or not they have a vocation to the priesthood or religious life, I would strongly suggest that they seriously consider taking part in the process or course entitled "Compass" at Worth Abbey in West Sussex, which is under the directorship of Dom Luke Jolly OSB. Participants in Compass meet together once a month for a year, in order to discern whether or not they have a vocation to the priesthood or religious life. This course has been going on since 2004 with encouraging results.

Of course such a vocation is contrary to the secular spirit of the age, with its emphasis on celebrity and fame, acquisitiveness and consumerism – things that rarely bring fulfilment. All told, I have no regrets whatsoever about how my life has turned out and do not hesitate to recommend priesthood to any man, young or old, who feels he is being called to be a priest.